Blessed José

www.blessedjose.com

Blessed José

Boy Cristero Martyr

Kevin McKenzie LC

Cover artwork by Margueritte M. Kenney
Photo Credit Page 206: Joel Castañeda LC

ISBN 978-1500420895
First Printing – November 2014

Printed in the United States of America

To Blessed José
In Gratitude

Contents

1

Spiral Stairs

"You two ready?" asked the priest as he scooped a heaping spoonful of incense onto the glowing charcoal.

It was late July, 1926. Sunday Mass in the small town of Sahuayo in central México was about to get under way.

"*Sí*, Padre," said the taller of the two altar boys, rubbing a hand through his mop of black hair. "This thing is so heavy." He shut the incense-laden censer with a clang. Its thick bronze rings dangled ponderously from the boy's fingers and the weight of the solid, heavily-filigreed censer made his hand droop slowly downwards. Smoke poured from its holes, wrapping the two boys and the priest in a heavy cloak.

"Ready when you are, Padre Ignacio," said the shorter, chubbier of the two boys, clasping a large processional cross to his chest.

"Alright then," said the priest, straightening his vestments. "José, keep that thing open so the incense can come out, and don't let it touch the ground. Trino, make sure you don't bang Jesus' head on the doorway." He smiled.

Together, they bowed to the cross and stepped from the sacristy into the main aisle. José walked in front with the incense, Trino followed with the cross, and Padre Ignacio took his place in the rear.

José kept his eyes glued to the smoking censer as it swung back and forth, letting out bursts of thick, perfumed smoke.

From behind he heard a whisper.

"Am I supposed to genuflect with this thing?" Trino asked.

"You just bow," replied José, turning his head.

Distracted now, he didn't notice the censer drooping precariously low. As they neared the altar, its metal base scraped the surface of the clay floor-tiles, releasing a high-pitched ring.

"Watch out for the step," whispered Padre Ignacio from behind.

Still startled by the noise, José pulled up on the chain. He was too late. The censer rammed into the granite step at the foot of the sanctuary with a deafening crash.

José watched with dismay as burning charcoal spilled from the open censer and scattered across the floor. Most of it landed harmlessly on the tiles, but one piece bounced its way to the rug beneath the altar. From where it came to rest, smoke billowed up.

"Fire!" cried a voice in the front pew.

"José, I thought you were gonna burn the whole church down," said Trino back in the sacristy, slipping the large cross into its holder.

The sound of chatter came from the back of church where a small crowd of women and children had gathered after Mass.

"Thank God for holy water," said Padre Ignacio, laughing, as he placed his large white vestment on a hanger.

Laughter filled the little sacristy. The two boys started taking off their altar server robes.

José turned to Trino and gave him a jab in the side. "Remember you were gonna ask…" he whispered, raising his eyebrows.

"*You* ask, José—it was your idea," snapped Trino. "Besides, he's *your* uncle."

"Oh, alright," said José, sticking a hand in his pocket. "Uncle Ignacio, have you ever been up in the bell tower?"

"Of course, José," the priest replied. "What makes you ask?"

"Well…um…you…see…uh…me and Trino— we've been wondering how far you can see from the top."

Padre Ignacio chuckled. "Why on a clear day, you can see all the way to the Cathedral in Guadalajara. That's over sixty miles away as the crow flies." A wry smiled crossed the priest's face. "Would you like to climb up?"

"Sí Padre, sí!" the boys blurted out eagerly in unison.

"Well then," said the priest, planting his toe and quickly wheeling around, "follow me!"

The boys tossed their server robes onto a table and followed.

Turning down a small corridor, Padre Ignacio brought them to a gnarled wooden door fastened with an ancient padlock. "Knowing you two," he said, fiddling with the keys, "there's more to this than just the view." He pulled the door open, revealing a spiral staircase.

José drew his hand from his pocket. Trino glanced at him, before speaking up. "Padre, there is a bet," he admitted sheepishly.

José rolled his eyes.

"A bet?" asked Padre Ignacio, arching his eyebrows. "What's at stake?"

"José says he can throw a rock from the top of the tower all the way to his house," Trino replied. "I say he can't. Whoever wins gets a pack of gum."

Padre Ignacio smiled. "How about we make a deal," he said. "I'll take you to the top of the tower... *if*," he raised his index finger and looked at them sharply, "if you leave your rocks at the bottom."

José cocked his head to the side, glumly. "Then who gets the bubble gum?"

"Look at the lake," said Trino, puffing from the climb. "It's all sparkling. I've never seen it from this high. Seems like it goes on forever."

"Papá says Lake Chapala is the biggest lake in all of México," said José, holding a hand over his eyes to block the sun. "He says that it used to be even bigger. Sahuayo was a lake town."

"I love Sahuayo just like it is," said Padre Ignacio, sighing. "Red-roofed houses, big trees—small but not too small—it's perfect." His eyes fell lovingly on the town square just below them, with its rows of cedar trees and the large iron gazebo in the center. "Our two churches—*Santiago* and the *Santuario*," he gazed across town to the other steeple, "—make Sahuayo something special. There aren't many two-church towns around."

The three figures gazed in silence. Swallows dipped and soared through the warm summer air. Higher still, fluffy clouds like wads of cotton candy drifted across the sky.

"Uncle Ignacio, is it true what they say?" asked José, breaking the silence.

"About what?" asked the priest.

"That President Calles wants to close all the churches?"

"I wish it wasn't true," Padre Ignacio said with a sigh. "Calles's new law will make all churches government property—"

"But that's not fair," José broke in.

"—and I won't be allowed to wear my cassock any more. I'll also have to get my homilies approved by the government. Priests can either become employees of the state, or leave the country."

"When's all that supposed to happen?" asked Trino.

"Next Sunday, August first."

"Why can't they just leave the Church alone?" fumed José. "It's like they want the Catholic Church to become a government business. Isn't there anything we can do, Padre?"

"Not really—short of all-out war. But the bishops have their own plan. If President Calles goes through with his law on Sunday, they've asked all of us priests to suspend public worship until further notice. They will turn the whole country against Calles. They want to send him a signal that life can't go on like this."

2

Shots in the Town Square

"Did you see the sign?" blurted Trino, sombrero in hand, as he raced around the corner onto Tepeyac Street.

José was sitting in the shade in front of his house. "What sign?" he asked, looking up at Trino.

The boy leaned heavily against the wall of the house, breathing in lungfuls of the warm mid-morning air.

"The sign in church over the tabernacle. It says '*No está aquí*': 'He's not here'."

José jumped to his feet. "The Eucharist is gone?" he demanded.

Trino nodded slowly and shrugged his shoulders in helplessness.

Suddenly, a loud boom split the stillness.

"What was that?" cried Trino, his eyes wide with fear.

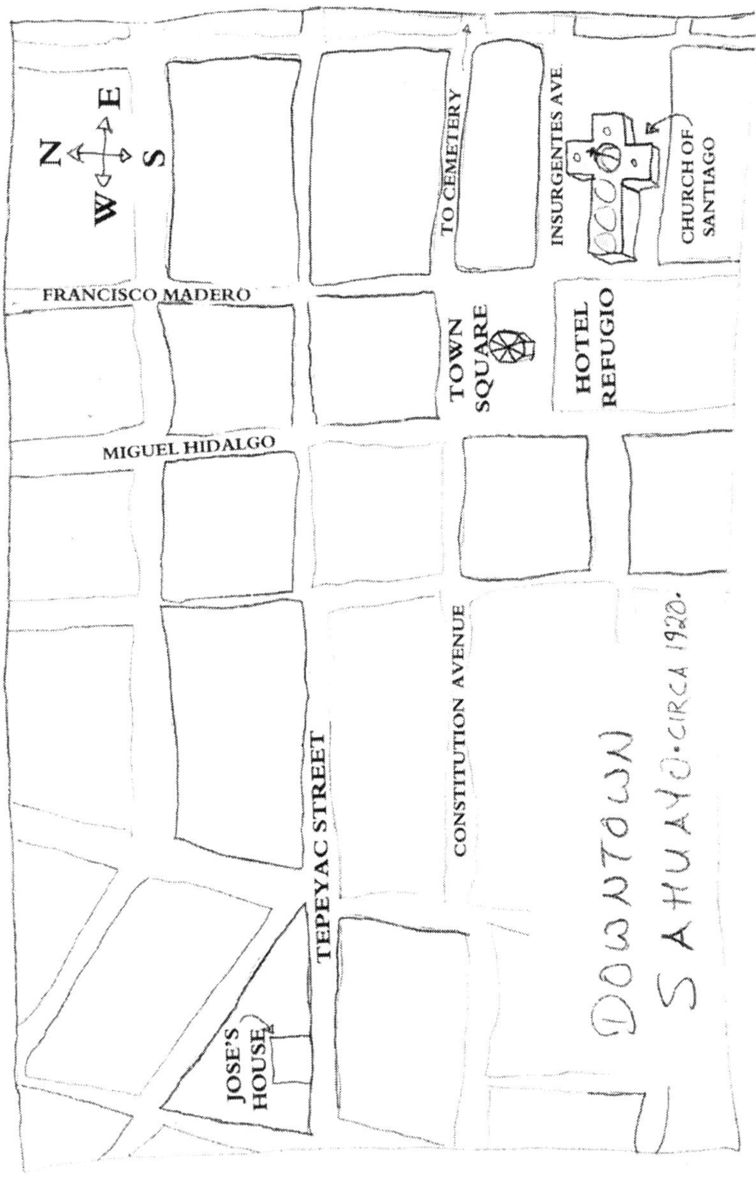
N
E
S
W
FRANCISCO MADERO
MIGUEL HIDALGO
TO CEMETERY
INSURGENTES AVE
CHURCH OF SANTIAGO
TOWN SQUARE
HOTEL REFUGIO
CONSTITUTION AVENUE
TEPEYAC STREET
JOSE'S HOUSE
DOWNTOWN
SAHUAYO · CIRCA 1920 ·

"I don't know," growled José, "that was too loud for a firecracker."

A minute later, another loud explosion shattered the dry air.

"Sounds like a gun to me," said Trino, "a *big* gun."

"Yes," added José, "and it's coming from over in the square. Let's go see."

"We'd better stay low," Trino cautioned.

"OK," answered José, "follow me."

As the two boys approached the square, an itching started to grow in Trino's throat. "José," he said, "Maybe we shouldn't do this—maybe we should just go home."

"I still think we should go and see," José replied. "Otherwise, we'll never forgive ourselves for being chicken. Come on, follow me. We'll crawl like we're soldiers."

"If you say so," said Trino, dropping to his knees.

The two slowly made their way down the last street before the square. Nothing moved on either side.

As they approached the end of the street, the square came into view. In the center rose the tall iron gazebo. To the south, directly across from where they crouched, stood the two-storied *Hotel Refugio*. To the left sat the church of *Santiago*, with its huge bell-tower looming over the deserted square.

"*Qué raro,*" José whispered, "There's no one out. Feels like Good Friday."

"I wish it *was* Good Friday," said Trino.

Another bang, this one louder than the last, broke the silence. It came from the direction of the big black gazebo.

"Look," said José. "It's Picazo—moustache man. And he's got help."

José pointed to a figure crouching down behind the gazebo. A large, black handlebar moustache was plastered across his face. Behind him squatted others, weapons in hand.

"You mean—" Trino was cut short by the crack of another gun from the direction of the Church.

"What was that?" asked José, dropping to his knee.

"Look, on top of the Church," pointed Trino. "Somebody's shooting from the bell tower. He's got a rifle."

"Are Picazo and his men trying to take over the Church," asked José. "*Diablos!*"

"I thought he was Catholic!" said Trino, shaking his head.

"At least he's not your *padrino,*" said José bleakly.

Trino slowly turned in surprise.

"You mean you're his..."

A loud burst of gunfire jerked his head back.

"It's a shootout," sputtered José.

The firing from both sides grew in volume. Too much was coming from the church for one man. The men stationed behind the gazebo kept firing sporadically.

As the shooting continued, José let out a gasp. Someone had opened the large front door of the church and slipped out to the left.

"It's Padre Ignacio," cried José. "What's he doing?"

"He must be trying to escape," said Trino.

The priest dashed left, black cassock flapping behind.

"How can he make it?" shouted José. The hail of bullets continued. They ricocheted off the ground and the wall of the church. Then suddenly, the black cassock stopped and came crashing to the ground.

3

To the Rescue

"No!" cried Trino. "No, it can't be. No!" Tears streamed down his face.

"Quiet," barked José, squirming in the dust and grabbing Trino by the shoulder. "Don't get *us* killed too."

"But Padre Ignacio—he's shot! Can't we do something?"

"Here," said José, "let's go around the block. Maybe we can reach him from behind."

Trembling now, Trino nodded.

The two retraced their tracks, backing away from the plaza. Once out of sight of the gazebo, they stood up and ran.

José's heart pounded against his ribs like a sledgehammer. Thoughts raced through his head. *No.*

No. No! It can't be. Not Padre Ignacio. What had he done? That creep, crook—Picazo—who does he think he is? Mamá will be terrified. Why doesn't anyone do something? Why doesn't somebody stop them?

The noon-day sun cast no shadows on the silent streets. Quickly they made their way south in a large loop toward the church. At Insurgentes Avenue, they headed toward the square. Near the end of the street, the bell-tower of the church of *Santiago* reared up on their left.

Slackening their speed as the square drew near, they hunched down low.

"Where's Padre?" whispered José.

A soft whistle came from the trees beside the church. The boys turned to look. At the base of a large oak sat a bundle of black.

"It's Padre Ignacio!" he said, stifling a shout.

With a flutter of his arms the priest beckoned the boys over.

They scanned the street for a moment. The gazebo and Picazo's gunmen were out of sight. They sprinted to the row of trees.

"You two have a nose for trouble," the priest joked, as the boys pulled up, breathless.

"Are you OK?" asked José, not noticing the humor.

The priest moved his right leg just enough to reveal a reddish circle in the dust. "They got me in the calf. Nothing a couple of stitches can't fix — I hope. I can still walk a little."

He planted one hand on the tree. "We've got to get away from the square. Here, help me up."

Each boy grabbed an arm. Soon they had walked the wounded priest to the end of the street.

"Enough, enough," he said wearily. "I'm out of danger now." The two boys lowered him to the ground in the shade of a building.

"Was that you back there, Padre Ignacio?" asked Trino, glancing up at the bell tower.

"What, you mean with the rifle?" he answered as his lips grew into a large smile. "No, that's Señor Guízar. He's got a scope too. Not that bad a setup. There are five men, all told. I wanted to stay, but they wouldn't have it—said a bottle of Tequila would last longer than I would if *los federales* ever got their hands on me."

José spoke up. "Padre, we've got to get you out of here. Want me to bring my horse?"

The priest scratched his head. "I don't know, I wouldn't feel safe that high up."

"How about a wheelbarrow?" asked Trino.

"That sounds better."

José stared at his uncle for a moment "If you say so," he said, "but you're in for one rough ride. Give us some time, and we'll be right back."

"Fine," said Padre Ignacio, "but be careful. Baptizing you was one thing; I'm not about to do your funeral."

José and Trino took off. They raced down Juarez Avenue until they hit Tepeyac Street.

"Should we sneak in the back?" asked Trino, struggling to keep up.

"No—waste of time," answered José, panting, as they neared the house.

"What if your parents stop us?"

"Papá will understand."

The boys ran up to a white-walled, adobe-roofed house. From the outside, nothing seemed to be stirring. José banged a fist on the large red door.

"You take one more step, and it'll be your last," announced a gruff voice from inside.

A long rifle barrel protruded from the window on their left.

"Papá, it's me, José."

Don Macario Sánchez poked his head through the window. His short white beard sparkled in the sunlight. "*Madre Santa,* where have you been?" he demanded.

Before José could answer, the front door swung open to reveal José's older brother Miguel. "Mamá has been scared out of her wits over you, José."

Stepping through the doorway he stood before his father, who still clutched his rifle. Trino followed.

"Padre Ignacio's been shot and he needs help."

The news fell like a bomb. "Padre Ignacio? Shot? What?" cried Don Macario, staggering backward.

By this time, the other children had started to gather behind their father. José heard shouts from further inside the house.

Don Macario strode forward and grasped José's shoulders with both hands. All color had left his face, but he recovered quickly. "Tell me exactly what happened, José."

"We were watching the gunfight in the town square. Padre Ignacio came running out of the church right in the middle of it all. They got him in the leg. He sent us to get a wheelbarrow so we could rescue him."

Don Macario pulled a red handkerchief from a pocket and wiped his forehead. "How is he? Is it bad?"

"He'll live. There's no time to explain Papá. We need to get back with the wheelbarrow—quick." José hurried by his still-astonished father and into the house.

Past the foyer and down the hall, the cry went up, "Shot! Shot! Padre Ignacio's been shot!"

José pushed his way into the courtyard, Trino at his heels. "Where's the wheelbarrow?" he cried. "Miguel, who moved the wheelbarrow?"

Frantically, both boys started running back and forth. Then José slapped a hand to his forehead. "Wait a minute. I know where it is." He hurried over to the chicken shed and pulled open the hatch. Birds and feathers went flying in all directions. "Just my luck—they've already turned it into a nest," he exclaimed, grabbing a handful of straw.

Trino helped him scoop the debris out. Then, carrying the wheelbarrow, the two friends took off back through the house.

"José," said a voice. A light hand touched his shoulder as he passed by the family room. Out of the corner of his eye José spied a long blue dress.

"Mamá," he said, pulling to a halt and gazing up into the dark brown eyes of his mother.

Teardrops glistened on her face. He set the wheelbarrow down. Laying one hand upon hers, he tried to explain, "Mamá, Padre Ignacio needs our help."

She nodded in agreement. "You take care of yourself, José."

He wrapped his arms around her, long black hair and all.

Picking the wheelbarrow up again, they wound their way through people and passageways, finally slipping out into the sunshine.

In the middle of the street stood Miguel and Guillermo. "We're coming with you," said Miguel.

"Good," replied José, smiling.

"Wait a minute, I'm coming too," said Don Macario, stepping through the doorway, rifle in hand. "No one's going to take another shot at my little brother."

4

Why

Later that night, the Sánchez del Río family huddled around the couch in their living room.

"Looks like I won't be visiting any sick people for the time being," said Padre Ignacio, giving his bandaged leg a pat. "This time, I'm the one that needs the last rites!"

"Not yet you don't," said Doña Mariquita, who held little Celia in her lap. "As soon as it's safe, we'll take you to Doctor Santos. You can hold out here as you are for a few days."

"I can hold out, but what about all these bright young minds I see?" asked Padre Ignacio surveying the children. "After taking over the church, first thing Picazo did was shut down the school."

"God have mercy on his soul," replied Doña Mariquita, wringing her hands. "And to think that he used to be our friend, that he still is José's *padrino...*"

"*Padrino* or not, he'll have a lot of reckoning to do when he comes before God," said Don Macario, fingering his snowy-white beard.

"I just hope Trino's alright," broke in José, who sat on the floor at the foot of the couch.

"Where did he end up?" asked Padre Ignacio. "As soon as you had me safe and in the wheelbarrow, he took off. I hope he doesn't fall into the hands of the federals. They already killed Señor Ramírez—without a trial."

"Trino told me he was going to check on his family. I sure hope he's okay."

Padre Ignacio nodded. Staring up at the ceiling, he let out a sigh, and said, "I wonder what they've done to the church."

"Couldn't anyone defend it?" asked José.

"Señor Degollado did his best. I hear that Amado died right in front of the main door. Even Lola held off Picazo and his gang for a little while. But when the army came, there was nothing to do. They set up their cannons on the hill, and from then on it was either give up or be blown up."

"I knew it was only a matter of time," said Don Macario, picking up his rifle from the corner, "until Picazo would come out of hiding and seek revenge. He's the kind that can't wait."

"He's also the kind that can't tell a jackrabbit from a rattlesnake," said Padre Ignacio. "He and his goons shot little Manuel, Señor Barragán's son, in the first few minutes of the fight. The boy was just trying to make it to safety."

"If these are the people that are supposed to be running Sahuayo," said Don Macario, fiddling with the sights on his rifle, "then the safest thing we can do is get out of town."

Silence fell. The rays of the setting sun played on the living room wall, and in the courtyard a rooster crowed.

"But why, Padre Ignacio," asked José, breaking the quiet. "Why do they want to take away our churches?"

Padre Ignacio straightened up. He patted the white gauze bandage wrapped around his leg.

"Why did they persecute our Lord?" he asked. "I think that's the important question."

"Well," said José, twining his hands together, "that's easy. It's because he wanted to change things—change things for the better." He looked hopefully at Padre Ignacio.

"Good," the priest replied. "Jesus wanted to start a fire here on earth, a fire that would wake people up. He wanted to deliver them from their slavery to sin and help bring them to heaven. But they didn't understand. His teachings made them feel uncomfortable. Many thought he was crazy," Padre Ignacio paused, and then slowly swept his gaze around the room. "If they wanted to kill him, should we – his followers – expect better treatment?"

Ever since México achieved independence," he continued, "there have been struggles between the Church and the government—but nothing like now. President Calles' new laws are meant to make the Church become just another arm of the state. He's even named his own 'Mexican Pope'. Now he's taking over all the churches. He's gone too far."

Padre Ignacio turned to look at José. The boy was staring dreamily at the rifle in his father's hands. Then he shook his head a moment, and said, "But—but Padre, isn't there anything we can do?"

"Yes there is," said Miguel, José's older brother. The tall, well-built boy clenched his fists. "We can fight back. I think we could beat them."

"I have my suspicions," said Don Macario, "that we won't have long to wait before somebody starts fighting the government. Señor Guízar is now officially an outlaw, as is everyone who helped defend the church today. He'll have to go into hiding, or fight. And there are others, though it will take more than just a few to stand up to President Calles and his cronies."

"Who knows what all the Catholics could do if they decided to resist?" said Padre Ignacio. "I think they don't know how strong they really are."

"I hope that there's no need to find out," said Doña Mariquita with a sigh. "Just give us back our churches, and we'll be happy."

The Calles Law of 1926

- No foreigners can be priests.
- Worship outside churches is prohibited.
- Religious education is prohibited.
- No priests or religious may direct schools.
- Taking religious vows is prohibited.
- All religious communities are to be dissolved, and community life is prohibited.
- Dressing like a priest or religious is prohibited.
- Any priest who says that the articles of the Constitution do not oblige under conscience shall be jailed.
- Priests are prohibited from criticizing laws in public.
- Freedom of the religious press is suppressed.
- All churches become property of the state.
- The government decides which churches remain open.
- All other properties, such as houses of bishops or priests, colleges, seminaries, and convents become property of the state.
- No religious association can own or use goods.
- No church may be built without authorization of the Secretary of State.
- All priests must register with the state government to obtain authorization.
- State authorities will decide the maximum number of priests that can minister within their territory.

5

Miguel

"Mamá, Papá, did you hear?" gasped the lanky figure catching his breath on the door step.

Several weeks had passed since the firefight in the town square.

"What? What is it son?" asked Don Macario. He had stood up from his chair in the living room as soon as Miguel, José's older brother, came dashing into the room.

Doña Mariquita's eyes darted from her husband to her son. José sat on the sofa.

"It's—it's Señor Guízar. He's not in hiding. He's fighting back," said the boy, struggling for breath. "He's joined up with Señor Ramírez."

"You mean José Ramírez?" asked Don Macario. "I know Picazo killed his brother, but I never thought Ramírez was the type to take up arms."

"It's not just those two. Señor Ramírez has about 300 men with him," said Miguel. "What's more, they have a name. They're called the *Cristeros,* because their cry is '*Viva Cristo Rey*'."

"'Long live Christ the King'—I like it," said Don Macario. "It's about time somebody fought back." He sat down and faced Miguel, now sitting on the floor with his back to the wall. "How did you find out about Señor Guízar?"

Miguel wiped his sweaty brow with a muscular forearm. "I was over at Adán and Guillermo's house. They're packing up their things right now so that they can leave first thing tomorrow morning. They've been accepted into the new army."

There was an uncomfortable pause. Miguel stared at his father.

"It's time," he continued. "I need to go fight."

"No!" came a shout from the couch. José had jumped up from where he sat.

Doña Mariquita glanced at Don Macario and rose to her feet. "I'll take care of this one," she said, heading through the doorway.

"Wait," said José, as she grabbed him by the shoulders and headed up the stairs, "we need to talk."

"And we *will* talk, just you and me," answered his mother, as they reached the top step.

"Are you really going to let Miguel join the Cristeros?"

"I don't know honey," replied his mother, tucking him into bed. "That's in God's hands."

As night slowly slipped away before the dawn, a lone figure dressed in a rusty-brown poncho scurried down the lane. Further back, on a doorstep, stood a man with a snowy-white beard. A woman in a long blue dress clutched his side. Her eyes tried to follow the figure in the poncho as he started down the hill to the city gates, but abundant tears melded everything into one big blur.

The face of a boy peeked out from the living room window. His fists were clenched into tight little balls and his eyebrows stood knotted hard together.

The figure in the poncho jumped into a cart drawn up against a house further down the road. As he covered himself with a blanket, the cart rolled off, and the muffled clickety-clop of the donkey's hooves ricocheted down the narrow dirt street. Then there was a bump and a "*Buenos días*" and they had cleared the city gates.

As soon as he was out of sight of the guards Miguel planned to slip from the cart and head off into the hills south of town. There he would meet up with his friends before joining the Cristeros.

6

Marbles

In the courtyard of the Sánchez del Río house, José knelt on the ground. Scratching his short black hair with his left hand, he leaned forward and placed the knuckle of his right hand on the ground, with the tip of his thumb tucked tightly behind a large red marble. Quickly releasing his thumb from his index finger, he sent the shiny little glass sphere careening through the cluster of marbles. It struck two smaller marbles, which in turned bounced out of the circle drawn in the dust. José herded them into his pile.

"Not bad," said Trino. "But not good enough. My smasher has been known to cause serious damage. Look."

Trino took aim and let his smasher fly. It bounced off the top of one of the little marbles and then landed outside the circle.

"Nice try," said José, holding his stomach and laughing.

Trino glared back at him.

"Hey, look on the bright side," said José. "At least your smasher didn't get stuck in the middle."

"Whatever," Trino muttered gloomily.

José straightened up. "Let's try this again," he said, launching his smasher once again.

This started a chain reaction, causing most of the smaller marbles to roll out of the circle.

"Did you see that?" José squealed with delight. He picked up his spoils—nine marbles in all.

Trino lowered his head in dismay and coughed. "Have you heard the news?" he asked.

José froze halfway through his victory celebration and stared at his friend. "No, what news?"

"The Cristeros are accepting boys our age into their army."

A stillness descended upon the courtyard. Even the chickens, sensing something was awry, ceased their usual clucking.

"Wait a minute, Trino," said José earnestly. "We're both thirteen, and you think they're going to let us join the army? My big brother went, but he was eighteen. Are you sure you heard right?"

"I know I heard right – it was a boy from Jiquilpan who told me."

They both went silent. On the other side of the courtyard, the clucking started again.

"What do you think?" asked José. "Think they'd accept *us*?"

Trino sat in silence. He turned to look at the chickens. "Your parents would let you go, wouldn't they?" he asked.

"I don't know."

José was fighting inside. *What would Mamá and Papá say?* he asked himself. *And do I really want to go? I'd miss my family...and army life would be hard and...I can think up a million reasons not to go.*

"How could we get there?" asked José.

Trino shrugged. "We'd have to write a letter to General Ramírez. Then, if he accepted us..."

"*If*," said José, "that's the question. Would they accept us? I don't know. But I know..."

Suddenly, José wasn't aware of his friend. He was five years old again, in the middle of the chaos of the Mexican Revolution. Don Macario was moving his family to the city for safety. The wooden cart rattled along beside the railroad tracks. Doña Mariquita gasped. Peering out, José saw things hanging from the telegraph poles—they were bodies, lots of bodies, as far as he could see. A blanket was thrown over his head and he saw no more.

Shaking his head and snapping out of the daydream, José looked around. "How about a *merienda*?" he asked. "I think there are some cookies in the kitchen."

7

Anacleto

The boy leaned all his weight against the heavy cathedral door, which slowly swung inward. Then he cautiously stepped over the threshold.

The massive slab of bronze swung shut, plunging everything into darkness. As he stood waiting for his eyes to adjust, he realized how nice and cool it felt. Then he noticed the faint light streaming from windows high above and piercing to the floor in golden shafts.

"Heaven on earth," he whispered softly.

As soon as his eyes could make out the pews and aisles, the boy walked over to the large round basin on the right and dipped his fingers into the holy water. With his hand still dripping, he made the sign of the cross. Then he lowered his right knee to the ground in genuflection.

As the dim outlines of the pillars and the high arches became clearer, the cathedral seemed to grow as if by magic. Now that he could see all the way to the altar at the far end, José realized that this was the biggest church he had ever been in.

Where was the tomb? His mahogany-brown eyes scanned the naves and aisles of the church. As he scratched his short black hair, he could barely make out the small side altars, votive candles, and statues of saints lining the walls. He took a few steps down the aisle, straining to see. Then the colors caught his eyes; there were flowers—bunches of them.

José made his way over. Someone had placed a long row of votive candles along the wall. In front, swathes of carnations, orchids, and roses covered the cathedral floor like a living carpet. Lifting his eyes to the wall, he saw a small bronze plaque:

VERBO VITA ET SANGUINE DOCUIT
ANACLETUS GONZALEZ FLORES

HE TAUGHT BY WORD, LIFE, AND BLOOD
ANACLETO GONZALEZ FLORES

It had only been a week earlier that Jose had heard the story from his uncle. The family had finished their after-dinner rosary, and Doña Mariquita had just taken the little ones off to bed.

"I'm going to tell you children about one of my good friends," began the priest. "His name is Anacleto

Gonzalez Flores. He was a top-notch lawyer—the best in Guadalajara."

When they closed the churches last July, he organized boycotts and tried to put pressure on the government to restore freedom of religion. But his attempts failed. When he offered to help the Cristeros, he instantly became a hunted man. In almost no time, the police raided the house where he was staying and put him in jail."

"Why, Padre Ignacio?" asked José, sitting on the floor at the base of the couch, "Why did they put him in jail?"

"Oh, mainly because he was helping the Cristeros, but also because he knew where the Archbishop of Guadalajara was hiding. He refused to tell them. So they tortured him. They hung him by his thumbs from the wall and whipped him. He wouldn't speak. So they took a bayonet and started to stab him."

José grimaced, as did the other children.

"When the police stopped their torture," the priest continued, "Anacleto wrote '*Viva Cristo Rey*' on the wall of the jail with his own blood.

"After receiving a terrible bayonet wound in the chest, he managed to gasp out his last words: "I die, but God does not die. *Viva Cristo Rey*."

Laying a hand against Anacleto's plaque, José slipped to his knees and began a whispered prayer: "Anacleto, I know you're in heaven because you died for Jesus. You had a lot of courage. I want to fight for God too, but I'm scared. The next time you talk to Jesus, please put in a good word for me. Tell him that I want to get to heaven to be with him. You, who are so close to God, please ask this grace for me."

He knelt in silence. Then, rising to his feet, he genuflected and headed resolutely toward the door.

8

Decisions

The very night of his visit to Anacleto's grave, as the Sánchez del Río family sat around the dinner table, José sat waiting for a moment of silence. They were all there—Doña Mariquita with the three girls at one end of the long rectangular table, and Don Macario down at the other end with the three boys. Next to José lay an untouched plate and an empty chair. They belonged to Miguel.

Several weeks had passed since he had snuck out of town in the cart. Shortly afterwards the family received a terse message saying he had made it safely to the Cristero camp and been accepted into the army.

In the center of the table sat a large basket of freshly baked bread and a pitcher of gravy. A bowl of steaming potatoes slowly made its way from child to child.

José eyed his chicken drumsticks. Picking up a ladle, he scooped some *pico de gallo* onto his plate. *Pico de gallo* was his favorite salsa—diced tomatoes, cilantro, onions, freshly squeezed lemon juice and peppers—it tasted good on most everything. He relished his chicken in silence. As always, Doña Mariquita's food was so scrumptious that words weren't necessary.

That's one of the things that keeps our family together, he thought, a grin spreading across his face, *mama and her food.*

Only the noise of forks and knives could be heard. The whole family was eating their meal with gusto.

I wonder if they'll say yes, José thought to himself. *Maybe they'll just send me to my room when I ask the question.*

Still chewing, he looked around the table at his sisters and brothers. *I'm going to miss them,* he thought. *Now that I'm ready to ask, I don't want to leave any of them. I wish I could take them with me.*

With the main course over, Doña Mariquita made her way to the kitchen. She returned carrying what looked like a squat amber-brown volcano with dark-brown syrup oozing down the sides.

"Flan!" squealed Celia, the youngest. The other children all smiled and fidgeted in their seats as Doña Mariquita cut the little volcano into slices.

José helped pass the pieces down to his father and his brothers, then he took his first bite. The flan was kind of like pudding, with a flavor like caramel, or toffee, but it was lighter, so you could eat more.

When everyone had scoured their plates, Don Macario stood up and headed through the big doorway at one end of the dining room which lead into the living room. One by one the children followed.

As they passed, Doña Mariquita handed out rosaries from a wooden cabinet.

"Hey, it's my turn," said José. "Mamá, Guillermo *always* gets the blood rosary."

"Well, if I remember right, you had it last night," replied Guillermo, "and the night before that, and the night before that." In his hand he fingered a rosary with deep-red beads.

"If you two bicker over rosaries here, I don't want to know what else you fight over," said Doña Mariquita with a sigh.

"OK, ok," said José. "We'll take turns—you get it first, and then we'll switch every ten Hail Marys."

Guillermo tossed his arms in the air. "Whatever, José," he said.

Don Macario looked at the boys. "If you're ready now, we'll begin. *Creo en Dios, Padre todopoderoso….*"

The children continued, "*Creo en el Espíritu Santo, la santa Iglesia católica….*"

They took turns saying the mysteries, and by the end, tired eyes drooped in tired heads as Doña Mariquita rounded up the smallest children for bed.

The older ones—both girls and boys—helped their father clear the dining room table. When they had finished, José followed his father back into the living room. Don Macario sat down in his big arm chair and pulled out a book. José stood in the opposite corner fumbling with his hands. *How should I say it?* he asked himself. *Is this the right moment?* His heart beat quicker. *If I don't go soon, Trino's bound to leave without me.*

"Papá," he said, sidling over and laying a hand on his father's knee, "Can we talk?"

Don Macario took off his reading glasses and turned toward his son. "Sounds like something serious," he said, smiling. "What's on your mind?"

José fidgeted a little and swallowed.

"Go on son, say it straight."

"Um, well, you know how Miguel went off to join the Cristeros? Well… uh… I want to be a Cristero too."

Don Macario didn't say anything. Setting down the book, he closed his eyes for a moment and drew his hands together. Wrinkles spread across his brow. He stroked his short white beard. Then he opened his eyes again and stared at his son before beginning to speak.

"José, your desire is very noble. God knows that the Cristeros are our only hope for peace and freedom now." He paused, and then spread wide his hands.

"But you're only thirteen. I wonder if any Cristero general would accept you."

Doña Mariquita had come down the stairs and was now standing beside her husband.

"Maybe if you wait till you are older—maybe then you can be a Cristero. I just don't see it happening now."

José leaned down closer to his father. "I thought the same thing too, Papá. But yesterday I was praying at Anacleto's tomb, and I felt that now is the moment. I feel stronger somehow."

José stood up and grabbed both his mother's and his father's hands. "Papá, Mamá, winning heaven has never been so easy. Now's my chance. I don't think I'll have another like it."

Doña Mariquita and Don Macario looked at each other.

Inside, José struggled. *I wish I had been born ten years earlier. Being thirteen always seems to be the limit. Why can't grown-ups understand that I can make big decisions too?*

Don Macario coughed a little. He nodded his head at Doña Mariquita, and then turned again to José.

"José, your mother and I had already decided this matter a long time ago. For us, there is nothing more important than God and his rights. The truth is, we support the Cristeros in as many ways as we can—more than you know. But we can't just let you run off to join the army—not at your age anyway."

I knew it, whispered a little voice inside José. *I shouldn't have even asked.*

Don Macario wasn't finished. "That's why we've decided that if a Cristero general accepts you, then you can have our blessing."

9

Letter Writing

"Dot your *i*'s and cross your *t*'s. Straight lines. Full sentences—hmmm. Capitalize the first words. Don't forget your accents."

José strained against the paper as he tried to recall his teacher's instructions from handwriting class. A pile of crumpled sheets lay on the ground. After seven false starts he was almost finished with his first letter.

"'Yours truly, José Sánchez del Río.' There." He gingerly laid down the pen and admired his masterpiece. All those hours of class had paid off.

General
Ignacio Sánchez Ramírez

Dear General Ramírez,

My name is José Sánchez del Río. I am fourteen and live in Sahuayo. My brother Miguel is a Cristero and I want to be one too.

If I am not old enough to handle a gun, I may be helpful in other ways, such as saddling the horses or carrying water and ammunition. And besides that, I could help with the cooking. I'll do whatever you need me to, just please, can I join your army?

José Sánchez del Río

"Looks good to me," said José. He carefully folded the letter and slipped it into an envelope.

"Now to find someone to deliver it." He slid out of the chair, grabbed the letter, and headed down the stairs.

As he made his way through the arched passageway, a delightful aroma caught his nose. His feet instinctively followed the fragrance to its source.

"Fresh *pan dulce*," he murmured, as he strode into the kitchen. His mother was pulling a sheet of small, pastel-colored cakes from the oven.

José felt his stomach growl. Summing up all the sweetness he could, he spoke up, "Mamá, do you think I could maybe have one *pan dulce*, please?"

Doña Mariquita eyed her boy. *This one sure has a knack for appearing at the perfect moment*, she thought.

"Where have you been hiding all this time?" she asked with a slight smile.

The letter in José's hand slipped back into his memory. "Oh um…I was writing to General Ramírez, and—" He paused as he saw his mother's face fall.

"Remember you and Papá said it was ok if I tried to get accepted?" José clutched the letter tight and barreled on. "Well, I need someone to deliver my letter to the Cristeros." He studied his mother's face. *She doesn't want me to go. I might as well give up now.*

When he looked again, he saw tears glistening in her eyes.

"Mamá…" his voice trailed off.

He stepped forward and stretched his arms around her—apron, *pan dulce*, and all. She set down the tray and hugged him back. They stayed that way for a long while. Then Doña Mariquita took José by the shoulders with both of her arms and looked straight at him through her teary eyes.

"Hijito mío," she said. "I don't want to lose you." She hugged him again, and ran one hand through his springy black hair. "I wish this war didn't have to happen."

Leaning her head back, she wiped the tears first from one eye, then from the other. After sniffling a bit, she continued, "No, you can't have any *pan dulce*." José looked longingly at the sweet buns and then back at his mother, who smiled. "I made them for the Cristeros. I'm taking them and some other food to their camp this afternoon. We can hide your letter in the basket."

José opened the door that led from the courtyard to the small stables behind his house. It squeaked on its rusty hinges. Immediately a loud neigh sounded from within.

"Don't worry Copper, it's me, José." The boy gingerly closed the door behind him and then tramped over to where the chestnut pony stood.

The horse was José's prized possession. He had raised it from a foal, and now that the animal was full grown, he rode it whenever he could.

Holding up his hand, José offered the animal a slice of apple. Copper took a sniff and then the fruit was gone.

José laughed. "You old magician, how do you do that without biting my hand off?"

Copper chomped away at the apple contentedly.

Pulling a brush from the wall, José stroked the horse's sides, combing out brambles.

"Copper, guess what? All this time I thought Mamá had been spending her afternoons over at the Espinosa's house. She always disappeared after lunch and wouldn't come home until dinner.

"But that was for show. She's really been secretly delivering food and supplies to the Cristeros. She takes turns with other ladies in the town. Picazo doesn't suspect them yet. She's going to take my letter today."

The horse didn't show much interest in José's tale. Instead, it was sniffing at one of his pockets.

"Silly horse. *Pan dulce* is bad for you. Mamá gave me one because she said it's to make up for all the sweets I'll miss if the Cristeros really do accept me. You'll need a lot of apples to make up for all the ones you'll miss too. We'll be going together."

Copper neighed softly.

"Let's see," said José. "I've got a horse. I think I have the clothes I need." He paused.

Copper whinnied.

"You're right," said José, grinning and giving the horse a pat, "all that's missing is a gun."

10

Picazo

In his roomy corner office on the town square, Rafael Picazo paced back and forth. As he walked, he stroked his shiny black handlebar moustache methodically.

The desk by the window was nearly as neat as the moustache itself. Made from mahogany, it was rich-looking, sturdy, and formidable. It made him feel powerful to sit in his tall executive chair and stare out at the people who came to him with their problems.

Being mayor of a town like Sahuayo wasn't normally an exalted position, but war had changed that. Rafael Picazo now had broad powers, if he chose to use them—life and death power over every inhabitant of the town.

But Picazo was worried too. As he smoothed the left tip of his shiny moustache, his eyes strayed yet again to the document on top of his desk.

Known Cristero Locations

He had thought that after he and his cronies stormed—and took—the town church, all his problems would be settled. The federal soldiers with their cannon had certainly made a big impression on the people. But the cannons were gone now, bringing "peace" to some other town.

According to the secret government document lying on his desk, Sahuayo was basically surrounded by roving bands of Cristeros. It appeared that none stayed too long in any one place, but the vast majority of them seemed to be hiding in and around the mountains to the south and east of town. *Just my luck,* he thought.

Ambling over to the far corner of the room, he stopped before a cabinet with an oval mirror. He eyed his reflection.

"What are you doing, Rafael?" he asked himself. "Are you fighting for a lost cause?" He nudged the left side of his moustache a little higher, balancing it out.

"No," he said, answering his own question, "this is a noble cause. I am fighting to preserve law and order from these vigilantes and their version of justice."

He fumbled with one of the cabinet drawers. Inside sat a box of cigars. The enticing smell of tobacco drifted up. Drawing a cigar out, he turned and strolled back over to his desk.

Another document on the desk drew his attention.

Known Cristeros

He leafed through the ten pages of names. Many were underlined in red ink.

"My own people — traitors." He spat into the trash can at his feet.

He had already set the papers back down, when a strange idea struck him. Picking the document up again, he studied the names in red. "Guízar... Galvez... Hurtado... Castañeda... Ochoa... Lopez..."

With each turn of the page, a slight grin began to worm its way across his moustached face. From time to time, his eyebrows raised a little.

When he had finished his survey, he laid the document down and let out a short laugh. "So stupid, these people. Ha! Stupid – and rich."

11

A Second Glance

A muffled knock came from the front door.

Doña Mariquita looked up from the book she was reading and listened. Thud, thud, thud. There it was again.

She got to her feet and made her way down the hall.

"Who's there?" she asked, ear to the door.

"It's me," said a voice. "Trino."

She undid the latch and the door swung inward. "Looking for José?"

The boy swept the sombrero off his head and gave a little bow.

"Sí Señora. Do you know where he is?"

"He stomped off to the courtyard after lunch," she said sadly. "He didn't like the general's answer."

"*Carambas,*" said Trino.

Doña Mariquita smiled and started down the hallway. "He must be with Copper. That horse of his has to be the most beloved animal in all of Sahuayo."

Trino nodded.

Opening the door to the courtyard, she gave a look around. "José, Trino's here," she called.

"Be there in a minute," answered a voice from the shed.

"Go ahead, Trino," said Doña Mariquita. "Merienda is at five."

"Gracias," said Trino, heading over to the shed. He poked his head around the doorframe.

Inside, José was running a brush down his horse's side. He stopped when he saw his friend.

"I heard the news," Trino said, as Copper sniffed at him.

José turned away and started brushing again without answering.

"Is it that bad?"

José nodded.

"The general said you can't go?"

"Sí," came the terse reply. The chestnut horse turned his head toward Trino and snorted.

"Wait a minute José. What did the letter actually say?"

"General Ramírez thinks that I would serve the Cristeros better by staying at home and doing nothing."

"Hmm... didn't he say anything else? Didn't he give you any options?"

"Not that I saw," replied José, setting the brush down. "Although I was so angry when I read the first line that—"

"—That you didn't read the whole thing?" finished Trino, stepping forward and laying a hand on the horse's side.

José shrugged his shoulders. "What use is there?" he asked, "I have my answer. I ripped the thing to pieces."

"As long as you still have the pieces we can put the letter back together—you know, like a jigsaw puzzle."

"If you say so," replied José, shrugging his shoulders.

"Of course I do. *Vámonos.*"

"First the four corners."

"First get your sombrero out of the way."

"You sure these are all the pieces?"

"I tossed them straight in the trash can when I ripped it up."

"Let's see what we have."

"That's his signature, big and flowery."

"Yeah… so these pieces go at the bottom. Here's your name – top left corner."

Both boys worked in silence.

Trino looked up from the puzzle they had pieced together. "That was easy," he said. "Let's see."

Dear José,

While I appreciate your offer of help, I think it better that you wait until you are older to join my regiment.

I doubt that any General would be willing to receive you at such a young age, especially here in the Sahuayo district.

"Especially here in the Sahuayo district," both boys repeated together.

"José, do you know what this means?"

"That I should have read it more carefully," said the boy, shaking his head.

"So what? You've got a horse, right? We'll have a lot better chance of being accepted by the Cristeros if we leave the 'Sahuayo district'."

"Hey," answered José. "Now that you mention it, I remember Papá talking about some Cristeros down by Cotija. Maybe we could join up with them."

12

Beginnings

José sat despondently on the three-legged chair in the living room twiddling his thumbs.

Mamá and Papá have been gone for hours, he thought to himself.

"Well, not hours, but long," he said aloud.

"Long is better than never," said a voice from behind. José turned and saw Don Macario step through the doorway, followed by Doña Mariquita.

After they had taken a seat, Don Macario spoke. "José, your mother and I realize that you want to be a Cristero soldier, and that's a noble thing."

He paused and glanced at his wife before continuing.

"But we still think you're too young to be fighting in battles."

Here it comes, thought José; *they're going to insist on my having written permission.*

"That's why-" Don Macario coughed, looked at Doña Mariquita, and continued, "-that's why we have decided to let you go under one condition."

José's face lit up. "Condition? Sure—anything. What is it?"

"We don't want you fighting until you've turned sixteen. So you can go, not as a soldier, but as a helper."

The smile on José's face shifted to a look of puzzlement.

"Do you think they'll still want me?" he asked. "The Cristeros need *soldiers*."

Laying a hand on José's knee, Doña Mariquita spoke, "They need all the help they can get—not just in the fighting. There's all the food to cook, horses to take care of, equipment that needs cleaning—there's plenty to do."

Don Macario nodded. "If they don't want you, you are to come back home immediately."

"OK," said the boy, eyes wide with wonder.

Doña Mariquita spoke again. "José, I know I've told you this before, but your father and I are only looking out for your good. We believe this is what's best for you."

He smiled, and stretched out his arms, wrapping them both in a big hug. "Alright," he said, squeezing hard. "When can I start?"

Your Mamá and Papá really said you can go?"

"That's what I was telling you, Tía Magdalena. Don't you believe me?"

"Of course I do, José. I just thought you might be trying to pull my leg."

"Not this time. I came to you because I need some advice."

The tall lady straightened up in her chair. "Don't get me wrong José. It's not that I don't think you can help the Cristeros—and they certainly need all the help they can get, God knows that. It's just—you're so young. I bring them supplies almost every day, and I haven't met anyone your age there."

"But those are the Cristeros of Sahuayo," said José. "I want to go to Cotija. Anyway, the worst thing they could say is 'no'. What's there to lose?"

"Do you think they'll accept you?"

José shrugged his shoulders. "I'm not sure, but I just have to try. It's my only chance. If I don't go and help now, we might never get the churches open again."

The boy sure has his heart set on this, she thought.

"Alright, I'll help."

José laughed.

"First things first," said his aunt. "Do you know how to get to Cotija?"

José shook his head. "It can't be that hard Tía Magdalena. If I get lost, I follow the signs, right?"

José's Aunt let out a long sigh. "Men—you're all the same. Always think you know the way, until you're utterly lost." She tossed her arms in the air and pointed a finger at her nephew. "Don't expect there to be signs anywhere. You, my little friend, are going to need a map."

"I'm not afraid of asking for directions."

"The first thing you should be wary of," she warned him, "is talking to strangers. Anyone who wanders about these days probably isn't up to any good. And you can't count on your luck to get you anywhere."

"OK, so I need a map," José ceded. "What else?"

"You'll need enough food to last you the whole journey, because you can't count on finding much along the way." She thought a little. "Then there's water—you'll need some canteens. You'll need something to sleep under—"

"Like the clothes on my back," José blurted out.

"Or so you think, until you get up into the mountains, and you wake up one morning covered in rain, or frozen-stiff like a block of ice."

"Really?" asked José.

"Really. The Cristeros have told me." She took her nephew by the shoulders and stared into his eyes. "You, my dear nephew, are a city-boy. You have many things to learn—like how to build a fire. Add a flint to your list."

"OK," replied José, scribbling on a wrinkled sheet of paper. "A map, food for me and Copper, canteens for water, blankets, a piece of flint—anything else?"

Aunt Magdalena shook her head. "That's all I can think of now. Better get to work."

"But how?" asked José. "I only have a few *centavos*, and most of the stores are closed now anyway."

"Let me see that list," said Aunt Magdalena.

José handed her the slip of paper.

"Hmm," she said, running her eyes up and down. "A map I can get. Food, you can find. A canteen—you'll have to buy that. I have a few spare blankets. Flint? Why don't you ask Chema?"

"Because I just gave Chema my last peso to buy my gun."

"Well, you'll have to find some more pesos. Maybe you can do some chores."

She paused and wiped her glasses with her apron. Then turning back to José, she added, "And come to think of it, you'll need to learn how to cook. Tía Maria can teach you that. Otherwise, you might spend all your time shoveling manure."

13

Odd Jobs

"Hey, careful, you're dripping paint on me."

"Whose idea was this anyway? I was all for going straight to Cotija."

"It was my Tía Magdalena's idea, and she's pretty smart," said José, grinning, as he slapped a large swath of whitewash on the wall.

Trino paused, looking down from the top of the ladder at José, who stood on the bottom rung. "How many of these odd jobs do we have to do?" he asked.

Oh, I don't know," replied José, chuckling, "as much as it takes to buy all our supplies."

"I'd give anything to play *fútbol* right now," Trino lamented.

"Me too," José agreed, continuing to paint. "Let's see, we've been doing odd jobs for about a week now. We swept my house and your house and Tía Magdalena's house. We cleaned out too many chicken coops—yuck. We picked up those pine cones. We sold my bottle cap collection—"

"And Nacho," interrupted Trino.

"And Nacho, your turtle," acknowledged José, "who would *not* have made a good Cristero."

Trino held his dripping brush above José's head.

José rubbed the paint out of his short black hair, and continued, "All in all, I like the painting most. I figure we'll have enough money by next Friday. Then we'll go to Cotija!"

"One more week," said Trino, dipping his brush in the paint can. "I don't know if I can make it that long."

"Sure you will," said José. "We'll be leaving before you know it. All we've got to do is finish this painting, and my Tía Magdalena will do the rest. She's the best."

"You're right about that," said a voice from behind.

The two boys turned around, sprinkling the floor with paint as they did.

"Tía Magdalena," José asked excitedly, "what brings you our way?"

Ignoring the question, she pointed at José. "For heaven's sake young man, what is that in your hands?" she asked.

José smiled. "It's a better paint brush, that's what it is," he responded. "I took an old broom and tied three paint brushes to it—three is faster than one."

"If there wasn't more paint on the ground than on the wall," said Tía Magdalena, hands on her hips, "I might call you intelligent."

José glanced at the tangle of white muck at his feet. "Uh oh," he said, embarrassed.

"Well, I didn't come to scold you." Sticking a hand in her satchel, she pulled out a wrinkled, weather-stained sheet of paper.

"I've got your map."

José winked at Trino.

"How did you do it?" he asked.

"I forced those Cristeros to make it. I told that young one who is chef's assistant that he could say goodbye to his fresh meat and vegetables if he didn't find me someone to make a map. That did the trick. General Ramírez himself drew this. He's the only one that knows the area well enough."

"You mean *the* General Ramírez, the one who won't accept me into his army?" asked José incredulously.

"A hungry man will do just about anything for food."

Trino and José laughed. Tía Magdalena smiled. Then she spoke again. "That reminds me. You two have to learn how to cook before you go. Tía Maria sent me here to get you. You can learn *frijoles, carne asada, maíz,*—you know—the basics. You may be too young to fight, but there's no age limit on frying pans."

"It's a shame," added Trino, reaching down for more paint.

Later that night, Don Macario sat with his son after dinner.

"Gosh," said José, rubbing his left hand. "Tía Maria is pretty tough for an old lady."

"I wouldn't call her old," suggested Don Macario. "After all, she's my little sister."

"Well she made it all look so easy: 'First you get your fire lit. Then you put the beans in the kettle. Make sure to stir the beans as they cook.' She grabbed the kettle like with her bare hand. When I tried, the handle almost cooked my skin off – that's Tía for you."

"A little burn won't hurt you," said Don Macario, fiddling with the bottom tip of his snowy beard. "You put some aloe on it, right?"

"Mamá did, but it still hurts."

"You'll need to be able to take a lot more than that if you want to be a Cristero, José."

"You're probably right."

"What's this map you were talking about?" asked Don Macario, changing the subject.

"Oh yeah," answered José, pulling the piece of paper from his pocket.

Don Macario whistled. "Excellent," he said, eyes glued to the map. "Whoever made sure knew his geography."

"Tía Magdalena says that General Ramírez made it. She forced him to."

"Tía Magdalena forced General Ramírez?" asked Don Macario incredulously.

"She threatened to stop bringing food."

"Ha, ha. Sounds like my little sister alright. Say, José, I've been meaning to give you something. Wait here a minute."

Don Macario stood up and headed for the stairs.

José studied the map while he waited. Though handwritten, it was packed with detail. In the northwest was the large outline of Lake Chapala, and next to that lay Sahuayo. Cotija sat toward the bottom of the sheet.

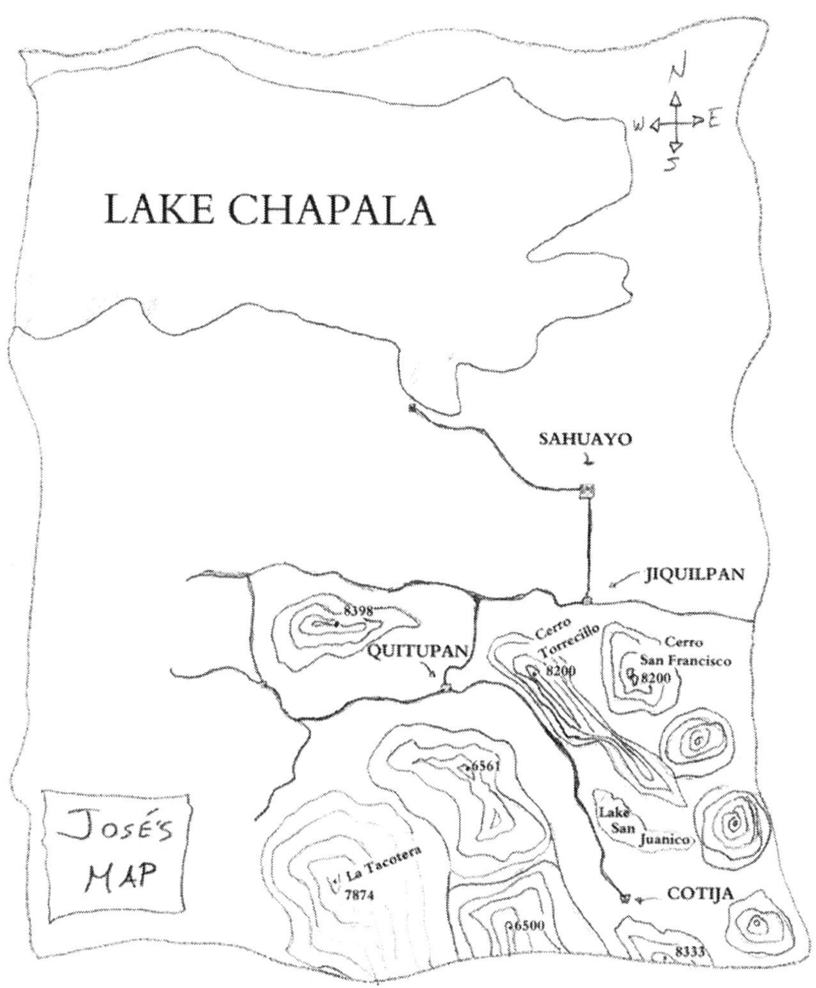

In between the two towns a few lines indicated country roads. These were crisscrossed by thicker squiggly lines—mountains, wild land where no one lived.

Don Macario walked back into the room. In his hand he held a small bronze-colored container.

"I haven't used this since my days on the ranch," he said, rubbing his fingers across the weathered surface of the object. "My father gave it to me, so I guess it's fitting that I give it to you."

He slipped off the metal lid of the small container. Inside, a needle floated, suspended on a point.

"This is a treasure," said Don Macario as he carefully placed it in José's hands. "They don't make them like this anymore. If you know where North is, you're never lost."

"Wow," said José, goggle-eyed. "For me?"

"You need it more than I do," replied Don Macario, reaching over and picking up the sheet of paper. "Let's go over this map. You'll have to learn how to use the compass properly before you go anywhere."

José nodded in agreement.

"As far as which route to take, I think fastest is best. Once you leave Sahuayo, you can skirt Jiquilpan and then follow the main road west. If you go under cover of night, the road should be clear. Just follow the signs to Quitupan."

"Wouldn't it be quicker to cut across the countryside and make straight for Cotija?" asked José.

"If these were plains, sure," explained Don Macario waving his hand across the bottom part of the map. "The problem is, you'd be heading straight through mountains. Who knows what you'll run into? Roads are the only safe way, especially at night."

"Well, I hope I can find my way in the dark," said José, head bent over the map.

"That's where the compass comes in handy. If you follow the contours of these hills—they are actually very detailed here—and if you use your compass faithfully, you can't miss the turns. Take the first right, then the second left after that, and you'll be in Quitupan. There's a regiment of federal soldiers stationed there, so you'll do best to keep low."

"OK. And after I get to Quitupan, I just head south through the hills, right?"

"Not hills—mountains. This one here, Cerro Torrecillo, is about 6,000 feet high."

"Wow, that *is* high."

"You'll take a left in the town square in Quitupan—everyone will be asleep—and then the road will take you along the base of these cliffs." Here he pointed to a row of narrow lines.

"After the cliffs let up, you'll come alongside Lake Juanico. If you skirt the lake from the south, you can't miss Cotija. It's not as big as Sahuayo, but still, it's a town. Where are you supposed to meet the Cristeros?"

"Tía Magdalena said they'd be in the mountains south of town. She said there are so many Cristeros there I'm bound to find my way to the general, if they don't mistake me for a spy and spear me first."

Don Macario looked skeptical. "They're not that stupid."

"I figure that if I make it to Cotija in one piece, then I've done pretty well," said José.

"Oh, I'm sure you'll make it there just fine," said Don Macario, yawning and glancing at his pocket watch. "It's past my bedtime now—and yours. Good night young man."

14

Pressure Building

"What would Anita and Adela say?"

"I don't care. I donate enough to my sisters' convent to keep them happy anyway."

Rafael Picazo and his wife Consuelo stood in Picazo's office overlooking the town square.

"But Rafael, it's like you've sold your soul away. You know deep down that what you're doing is wrong, don't you?"

"Consuelo, there's nothing I can do," the man answered, giving a tug on his handlebar moustache. "I'm an employee of the government. Orders are orders, and they've ordered me to take over the churches. Do you want our children to go hungry?"

Who is this man I am talking to? thought Señora Consuelo. *Fifteen years ago he would have been quick on his feet to bring the children to Mass and the rosary. But now—my husband is not the same.*

"Rafael, to tell you the truth, at this point I'd rather the children go hungry than have their father destroy himself like this."

Picazo frowned at the wall, clenched his fists, and turned, snarling, "Last time I checked, I was still the head of this household. Your job is to take care of the children. My job is to make a living."

Turning abruptly, he slammed the door and stormed down the hall.

"She's right," mumbled Picazo as he tramped along. "But how can I get myself out of this trap?"

The courtroom scene years ago played itself out again in his head. He was in the witness stand. A friend in politics had promised him a good job if he would say what they told him to say in the trial of an elderly priest. Halfway through his false testimony, a man strode into the courtroom. It was the accused priest. Realizing his bluff was called, Picazo jumped from the witness stand and fled the room. The priest was acquitted, but Picazo got his position.

"I don't hate the Church," he mumbled as he closed the door of his office behind himself. "I just have to do my job."

15

The Journey

The tips of the solitary hedge shone emerald green in the rays of the dying sun. Sahuayo had seen its fair share of gorgeous weather the whole month of June. Cool nights had been followed by pleasantly warm days with crystal-clear skies. Now a tremulous breeze tugged at the trees and bushes.

The hedge shook a little as a cloak-draped figure poked his head through a gap in the leaves. Dragging behind in his left hand were the reins of a pony.

The figure stood still for a moment, surveying the surrounding plain. All was clear. The only movement came from the swallows that dipped and plunged through the air overhead.

"Where's Trino?" José asked his horse.

Turning, he peeked into the bundle on Copper's back. His canteen, Trino's, their blankets, food, the map—everything was just as he had packed it. The two revolvers still lay well-hidden at the bottom.

The horse whinnied, giving José a start.

"Easy boy, he'll be here soon."

Just then a rustling came from the hedge, and José turned in time to see a head peek through.

"Is the coast clear?" Trino whispered.

"What took you so long?" asked José impatiently.

"I was saying goodbye," said Trino, pulling himself through the hedge.

By now the grey dusk had begun its slow advance across the plain. In the southwest, just above the mountain tops, a vivid red filled the sky.

"I hope your horse can see well in the dark," said Trino.

"Oh, I'm hoping we don't reach the tricky part till sunrise," answered José.

Slipping his foot into the stirrups, he gave a soft grunt and lifted himself up into the saddle. Turning to Trino, he leant over and gave him a hand up.

"Tough saying goodbye?" asked José, once they were both seated atop the horse.

Trino nodded. "Sí."

"Me too," said José. "Felt like I was leaving my heart behind."

He swallowed and then gave the reins a squeeze. "No matter. Ready?"

"All set," said Trino, managing a grin.

"Alright then," said José. He bent down to Copper's ear. "OK buddy, now's your chance. We have to get to

Cotija by tomorrow afternoon. Thirty miles—you can do it."

Copper needed no whip. He cantered off in the direction José pointed.

As the horse made its way across the flat toward the hills, José turned and watched Sahuayo growing smaller in their wake.

Turning forward again, he lowered his head until it was level with Copper's. The horse strained and pushed as it gobbled up the ground beneath them.

"You sure?"

"Look, my Papá said second left."

Skirting the town of Jiquilpan had been easy. The last light of dusk was just enough for them to see their way without being seen. Now they advanced by the light of a waxing moon.

"But where's the sign for Quitupan?"

"I don't know—never been there. But this has got to be it. All those other roads we passed looked like mule-paths compared to this one," said José.

He pulled the reins to the left. Copper continued forward a little, as if he didn't want to turn. José kept pulling until the horse reluctantly swung its head to the side.

Unlike the main road, here trees drooped over them, casting shadows on the already scant light.

"I hope Copper can see better than I can in this dark," said José.

"I don't have a good feeling about this," said Trino nervously.

José noticed movement ahead. He straightened up in the saddle and leaned forward to get a better view. Just then, something whacked him in the forehead, and he came tumbling off the horse.

Trino grabbed at the saddle, barely managing to stay atop the horse. Copper came to a halt.

"José, are you ok? What was that?"

"I don't know," came a weak voice from the darkness below.

"Here," said Trino from the horse, "Let's see what you hit." He fumbled around in his pockets and drew out a small matchbox. Taking a match between his fingers, he flicked it quickly against the back of his front teeth.

Holding the flame over his head, he whistled softly. "The branches are real low here. You must have hit one."

"Feels like it," said José, rising to his feet. "How does my forehead look?"

Trino held the match up to José's face. "Aw, it's just a scrape," he said.

"Good thing," said José, laying a hand on the saddle. "Why don't we uh… why don't we go back to the main road?"

"Now you're talking," said Trino.

José grabbed the loose reins just as the match sputtered out. "I think I'll walk Copper back," he said, "just to be on the safe side."

A couple of miles down the main road they came across the sign for Quitupan.

"Told you so."

"I know, I know. I've got the bump, ok?"

"It's your first battle scar," said Trino.

"Now you're talking. We can say that we were waylaid by bandits and I fought them off bravely," said José, guiding Copper to the left.

"And that you woke up from your dream when a branch whacked you," said Trino, chuckling.

A hush accompanied the darkness all around them. Neither beast nor man stirred on the dusty road to Quitupan. Mile after mile they trotted along in silence.

Then, ever so slowly, the path grew clearer again. A faint light came from behind them to the east. The sound of birds chirping reached their ears. Soon the color on the leaves started to return, faint at first, and then steadily building with every twist and turn they took. Heading round a curve between two eroded cliff walls, a few feeble rays of sunlight struck them on their faces.

Ridges and valleys riddled the country here. A light fog huddled in the low spots, and when they came to the top of a hill, they could spy an endless procession of wooded ridges thrusting up through the mist.

Here and there a grove of pines reared its head up as if in defiance of the smaller trees. Besides these little eruptions of branches, the land was covered with a uniform carpet of green.

Crossing over a small stream, they approached a wall of fog.

"I don't like the look of this," said José.

"Fog's better than dark," said Trino.

"If you say so."

Copper plunged in. A second later, looking back, Trino couldn't see more than ten feet away in any direction.

Fortunately, the trampled mud and grass of the road stood out clearly from the surrounding fields.

The horse didn't need any guiding. It followed the twists and turns just as well as the straight parts. José let the reins droop low.

As they rounded a wide bend, a soft ringing of bells came drifting over the wind. José pulled Copper to a halt and listened, peering through the fog.

"I'll bet they're cows. Can't mistake that smell," he said.

"If there are cows, there's bound to be a farm nearby," said Trino. "I'm starving. Maybe we can borrow some milk."

"Borrow? I kind of doubt we'd ever give it back."

"*Tonto*," said Trino, shaking his head. "You know what I mean. I'm going to go ask for some milk. You can stay here if you want."

"OK."

With a flick of the reins Copper started moving again. José steered him in the direction of the bells. Soon a fence materialized from the fog, and Copper bent his course alongside it.

Just ahead, a dark shape loomed up.

"Looks like a farmhouse," said José.

"Whatever happens, be careful," said Trino. "We don't want to blow our cover before we meet the Cristeros. I'm Pancho and you're Pepe, and we're going to Cotija to help Grandpa plant the crops."

José nodded.

They could now see the whitewashed walls of a building. The only door in sight was open, and light streamed from within.

"Let me do the talking," said Trino, as he slipped off the horse's back and landed on the ground.

José jumped down after his friend and led Copper by the reins.

Trino rapped on the house with his knuckles. There was silence. After a moment, he knocked again and gave a loud, "Anybody home?"

Noise came from their right, and both boys turned to see what it was.

Into view came the back of a tall skinny man dressed in a tattered grey cloak. He was pulling on a rope, which, they soon saw, was tied around the neck of a donkey. Strapped atop the donkey was a towering stack of rifles.

17

More than a Glass of Milk

When he had drawn up close, the man stopped pulling and turned to face the boys. He looked them up and down and then spat to the side—chewing tobacco.

"Good morning, strangers," he said, lifting his hat. "I'm Señor Chávez."

Thump, thump, thump, went José's heart. The bridle trembled in his hands. "Uh..." he began, trailing off.

"I'm Pancho," said Trino, stepping forward.

"Uh… and I am too," said José. A sharp jab between his shoulder blades made him wince. "I mean… I'm here with Pancho. My name's Pepe."

"We're uh, we're trying to find Cotija, and we were looking for some milk," said Trino.

"Milk I have," said the man, eyebrows raised quizzically. "But it's awful strange to find two youngsters on the road at this hour. Might I ask your business?"

"We're going to Cotija—" began Trino, "We're going to Cotija to help plant crops—"

"—Cristeros," blurted José.

Another sharp jab. This time José gave a yelp.

"You two alright?" asked the man, head cocked to the side. "My wife tells me I'm losing my hearing, but... you say you're going to Cotija to plant *Cristeros*?"

"To become Cristeros," said José, stepping forward. "I'm José and this is Trino, and we're going to Cotija to join the Cristeros—if they'll have us."

"My, my," said the old man, scratching his white hair.

"And we'd like something to drink."

At this, the man nodded. "Alright then, follow me," he said, turning around and towing the donkey behind him.

"I'm going to *kill* you," muttered Trino beneath his breath.

José waved a hand.

After tying up the donkey, the man turned and said, "Give me a moment to let my wife know we've got company."

He stepped inside.

"Now what?" asked Trino, throwing his arms up.

"What do you mean?" replied José, staring at the pile of weapons. "Are you scared?"

"If I'm here, it means I'm not scared. I just don't think—"

Señor Chávez came striding out the door and onto the porch. Leaning over the railing, he spat into a bucket and waved them over.

"Come on in. You boys need breakfast? My wife says you're welcome to a bite if you'd like."

José laid a hand on his stomach and smiled. Then he bounded up the steps to the house. He stopped before the doorway, turning. "What about my horse? He'll be hungry too," he asked.

"I could give him a little something to eat, if you want," said the man. "Appears he's traveled a lot recently."

Trino nodded as he handed the reins over.

The old man led the animal to where the donkey stood tethered. "You two run along to the kitchen while I take care of these good creatures."

Trino gingerly made his way up the steps and through the open doorway. José had already stepped inside. Trino paused, hesitating on the threshold, half expecting to see a potato sack drop over his friend's head. But nothing happened, so he plunged into the house as well.

"So you left Sahuayo last night and came all the way here on horseback?"

"*Sí Señora*. It was awful dark most of the way."

"That was because you were staring at my back," said José.

Ignoring the remark, Trino continued. "We almost got lost too. If it hadn't been for my bravery—"

"Ahem, 'bravery'?" interrupted José, as he slathered creamy yellow butter onto a slice of freshly baked bread.

Trino took another swig from a glass of frothy milk. "Call it what you like, I did find the right road," he said, licking his lips.

"There *is* some truth to that," José admitted.

Señora Chávez had sat the two boys down to a rough wooden table as soon as they stepped into the kitchen. When her husband walked in from tending to the animals, he found them up to their necks in fresh bread, jam, and milk. As they finished, Señora Chávez brought out a steaming platter of *chilaquiles*: tortilla chips with pulled chicken smothered in salsa, sour cream, and black beans.

Both boys piled their plates high. Trino cocked his head and gave José one of those looks that say, "Not bad when you're banking on stale tortillas."

"So, you're headed to Cotija?" asked Señor Chávez.

José was in the middle of twisting and inserting a heavily laden fork sideways into his mouth, and it barely fit. Still chewing, he attempted a feeble response. "Buhh," was all he could say.

Trino's cheeks bulged as he attempted to gulp down the *chilaquiles*. Huge drops of sweat bathed his face, certain price of the habañero salsa. He shook his head vigorously at Señor Chávez.

After a little while José managed to clear his windpipe enough to speak. "Sí. We're going to join the Cristeros."

Trino didn't protest the revelation this time, intent as he was on his plate.

Señora Chávez, who had finished cleaning up from her cooking, sat down across from José. "Aren't you boys a little young to be doing something like that?" she wondered aloud.

Setting down his breakfast-laden fork, José answered, "Yes, that's what most people say. And it's not like we've been accepted into the Cristero army yet. But it can't hurt to try, right? There are plenty of things we could do to help."

"Excuse me if I ask, but you didn't run away from home now, did you?" asked Señora Chávez.

Trino shook his head energetically. "No, no, no. My Mamá and Papá said I could go. I promise." He hastily jammed another overloaded fork down his throat.

José spoke up, "My parents said I could go too. It was tough for them, but they have a lot of faith, my parents. After that, all we had to do was get our supplies together and figure out a route to Cotija. Which reminds me, how do you get to Cotija from here?"

"I'll show you the way, when you're ready," said Señor Chávez. "Just take your time now and finish that breakfast. You'll need your energy for the journey."

"I'd say you'll reach Cotija by early afternoon."

After they had finished eating, the two yawning boys had reluctantly accepted Señor Chávez's offer of a place to nap. By the time they had awakened, cleaned up, and thanked Señora Chávez for breakfast, the sun was high in the sky. Now they sat atop Copper listening to directions.

"The quickest way is to take a left out of town here, and then follow the road as it winds along the base of the cliffs of Cerro Torrecillo. If you take a wrong turn you'll end up in La Maquina or Emiliano Zapata. That would add an extra three or four hours to your trip."

"Aren't there any signs?" asked Trino.

"Not that I remember," said Señor Chávez. "But there aren't many roads either, so it's hard to take a wrong turn."

"We've got a compass, so we can follow that south," said José.

"That might help. Once you come to Cotija, I suppose you know where to find your friends. Have a safe trip." He waved them on their way.

"You could have got us killed; that guy might be on the federal side," railed Trino once they were out of earshot.

"But I didn't. And we're still alive, aren't we?"

"Alive for now. But we have to be extra careful."

"I think it was all worth it for that breakfast," said José, adjusting the reins. "Those *chilaquiles* sure were something."

"True," said Trino, straightening his hat. "And after last night's ride, I was so sore. Guess I'd better get used to horses."

José shrugged. "That's *if* the Cristeros accept us."

18

Passing the Pickets

A golden sun was already sinking behind the hilltops when José and Trino finally made it around Cotija. They had decided not to risk cutting through town.

Once past it, finding their way had been difficult.

"You mean the general didn't tell you *where* to meet up with his army?" Trino asked.

"He's not going to tell anybody the exact location of his troops," José replied. "My Tía Magdalena said that once we're south of Cotija, the Cristeros will be in the mountains—pretty much all over the place."

"I sure hope we find them soon—seems like only coyotes would live in a place like this."

Just then, three bayonets flashed in the setting sun. Now the two boys sat at gunpoint atop the horse.

"Who lives?" demanded a voice.

José had pulled Copper to a halt as soon as he saw the rifles. Now he loosened up a bit on the reins. Before him stood three men dressed in dark clothing. All wore double bands of bullets crossed over their chests. The man who had spoken wore a collared shirt.

"Christ the King lives—*Viva Cristo Rey*," José replied, guessing this was the countersign.

"What is your business?" asked the man, lowering his weapon.

A sigh of relief escaped José's lips. "We're looking for the general… We, we want to be Cristeros."

"Give me your names, and where you are from," he said.

"I'm José Sánchez del Río, from Sahuayo."

"I'm José Trinidad Flores Espinosa, but they call me Trino."

"I don't care what they call you," barked the soldier. "We have no orders to accept boys into the army. How am I supposed to know you're not spies?"

"We're not, I promise, we can explain everything to the general," said José.

"Show me your credentials."

Both boys stared at each other in bewilderment.

"Credentials?" José asked.

"Yes, your documents."

"We don't have any… but my brother Miguel is a Cristero in Sahuayo, and my Mamá, Doña Mariquita, brings them food and supplies."

At this, the soldier glanced at his fellow soldiers. "You may be telling the truth, or you could be lying," he snapped. "Why should I let you pass?"

José straightened up in the saddle.

"Because I didn't come to play games; I came here to fight in the army of Christ the King," he declared.

The soldier grunted. Stepping aside, he drew another soldier—who limped as he walked—with him. They started talking quietly. The third man kept his rifle trained on the boys.

When they had finished, the soldier in the collared shirt spoke again. "We'll let you pass, for now. You will follow private Mijares here," he said, pointing to the soldier who limped. "But first, you must surrender any weapons you have."

José breathed a sigh of relief. He turned to Trino, who fished around in the bundle behind him until with an "aha" he drew out their two shiny pistols. These he handed to José, who passed them down to the officer.

"Do as private Mijares says, and speak clearly to the general," said the soldier. "And God go with you."

Mijares saluted the officer and hobbled his way over to a waiting horse. Once mounted, he beckoned to the boys, who followed him past the picket line. He kept an easy pace.

Darkness was now lengthening across the forest. José couldn't make out any path, though they seemed to be heading uphill mainly. It was just as well that they had someone to lead them.

Once over the brow of the first hill they slipped silently down into a valley. Here a blanket of moss carpeted the ground, except for some places where leaves had piled up in small drifts. Across the valley's bottom ran a stream. When they reached it, the soldier led them to a shallow place where the horses could walk across.

The trees cast inky shadows all around them.

"Who goes there?"

The words caught José off guard. They were still deep in the forest, with no camp in sight. Another picket?

"Viva Cristo Rey. Private Mijares here. Lieutenant Gódinez sent me to bring these two boys to the general."

A lantern-beam splayed out across the three. "Oh, it's you, Mijares," said a voice. "Who did you say you brought with you?"

"Two boys who want to talk to the general."

"Are you certain of their identities?"

"Why don't you ask them?" said private Mijares impatiently.

The soldier with the lantern didn't say anything as he looked the boys up and down.

Never thought I'd have to explain myself to so many people, thought José. *If only they would have accepted me in Sahuayo.*

"Explain yourselves," demanded the soldier.

"I'm José and this is Trino. We're from Sahuayo. We want to be Cristeros. We're looking for the general."

Noise came from the darkness behind the lantern. It was laughter. A smile appeared on the soldier's face.

"You know we have an age limit, don't you son?" he asked.

José felt his forehead turning red.

"You have to be sixteen to fight. How old are you, ten? Why don't you go back home and take care of your mother?"

"Actually, I'm thirteen, and I didn't ask to fight. I just want to help. The general will understand – I am sure."

"I wouldn't be so sure about the general. It's not that I hold anything against you, son, it's just that facts are facts. The youngest man in the army right now is seventeen."

José bit his lip. *I'm not about to give up here,* he thought.

"I understand what you're saying," he told the soldier. "We are young. But we still want to try. The worst thing the general could do is send us back home. If that's what he decides," José paused before continuing, "we'll do it."

In the dim light cast by the lantern, José saw the soldier rubbing his stubbly face. The lantern swung to the side for a moment as he glanced at those behind him.

Then facing the boys again, he sighed. "Alright then. You still have to get past the third picket anyway, and García is a stickler. Good luck."

"I'm sorry, but the general's got enough on his hands already. He can't spare time for two boys."

José sat speechless atop his horse. *He can't turn us back after all this, not at the third picket,* he told himself.

The soldier seemed to enjoy asking questions.

"So you come from Sahuayo?"

"Yes sir."

"And you left yesterday morning?"

"That's right."

"Where did you spend the night?"

"Near Quitupan. A family gave us breakfast and a place to sleep early this morning."

"Which family?"

"The Chávez family," replied José, as he fidgeted with the reins impatiently.

The soldier stiffened up.

"Chávez! What?"

Before José could answer, the three sentries had stepped back, forming a tight knot. Every now and then a man would wave an arm in the boys' direction. One of them flagged private Mijares, who joined in their discussion.

Baffled, José turned to Trino. "What did I say?"

Trino held up his hands in puzzlement. "Beats me."

After a heated discussion, the soldiers broke up and returned to their positions.

"Private Mijares will take you to headquarters now," barked the soldier in charge.

José shook his head in disbelief.

"And you'd better tell the general the whole story," growled the man.

One of the sentries stepped forward and quickly tied Copper to the saddle of Private Mijares' horse.

Trino shook José by the shoulder. "What's wrong?" he whispered.

"I have no idea," replied José, as Private Mijares started off.

19

In the Cristero Camp

Mijares led the boys at a snail's pace through the forest. Darkness seemed to fill the very gaps between their eyes. Eventually a steep hill rose up before them. The higher they went, the more the incline grew. Once over the brow of the hill, lights appeared in the distance. The horses paused a moment from their exertions.

Looking down, the boys could see a valley lit with many fires. They were shaped like two large circles meeting in the center.

"Follow me close," said private Mijares.

As they began the descent, the wind carried the sound of voices to their ears. It wasn't shouting or singing, just quiet voices rising and falling in the night.

Drawing nearer, they could make out the individual bonfires, each encircled by a ring of men. As they approached the first fire, a hush fell and many eyes turned to face them. "That you, Mijares?" shouted one of the men. "Shouldn't you be on picket duty?"

"Business for the general," he replied curtly.

They kept moving, zigzagging their way through the tents and fires, causing quiet to descend on those they passed.

Private Mijares stopped before a tent that was larger than the others.

"Stay here," he told the boys.

Dismounting, he limped over and saluted a guard standing just inside the tent's shadow.

"What's he saying?" asked Trino.

"I guess he's telling them who we are."

"If the pickets let us past, the general should accept us, right?"

José shrugged. "Let's hope so. If not, we'll have a long ride back to Sahuayo, or maybe—"

Private Mijares came hobbling back from the entrance to the tent. Climbing up on his horse, he motioned to the boys. "General Prudencio will talk to you tomorrow morning," he stated matter-of-factly. "We'll get something to eat now."

José opened his mouth to speak, but Mijares was already guiding them down a small incline. At its foot, they pulled up before a long wooden post at which other horses stood tied.

"The kitchen's on the other side of that fire," he said, pointing. "We'll tie up the animals here."

"What about food for them?" asked José.

"Let's look for food for us and them."

The three set off into camp. Scores of tents stretched away in all directions. As they walked, José noticed that most of the tents formed circles, and in the open spaces sat the campfires.

Many of the men were slowly making their way back to their tents, and some hailed them with a hello, or a good night, before continuing on their way.

Private Mijares escorted them to a largish tent with no sides. Piles of crates formed its chest-high walls. As they walked up to the entrance, voices came from within.

"I'm telling you, we need more meat," said a deep voice.

"Look, I'm just the go-between. I give you what the women give me, " said another voice.

"Well then, we'll have to send these soldiers out to hunt for deer and rabbits. The Lord knows they can't live off vegetables much longer."

Private Mijares limped up to the tent, and the boys followed.

A slim-looking soldier stood in the middle of the opening. At his side on an upturned pot sat a short plump man in white.

"Well what do we have here?" asked the plump man, hopping to his feet.

"Some hungry mouths to feed, if you have any leftovers," answered private Mijares.

"Why of course," replied the man in white with a sweeping bow. "Let me introduce myself first. I am Chef Gustavo. Welcome to my kitchen."

"I'm José Sánchez del Río, from Sahuayo."

"I'm José Trinidad Flores Espinosa, and I'm from Sahuayo too."

"Sahuayo, eh?" said the cook, turning and heading back among an assortment of kettles and boxes. "You don't happen to have any extra chickens there, do you? If you ask me, this vegetable stew could certainly use some."

José chuckled. "No, we're low on chickens too," he said.

As the boys sat themselves down on the boxes, the cook held up a pot and asked, "When was the last time you ate? You haven't come all the way here on empty stomachs, have you?"

"Not quite," answered José. "This morning in Quitupan Señora Chávez fixed us some terrific *chilaquiles*."

The clatter of pots and pans went silent.

"You said *what*?" asked the chef, a look of alarm spreading across his face.

"*Chilaquiles*," said José, looking from one man to the other. "They were really tasty." Still confused, he added, "What do you have against *chilaquiles*?"

The thin soldier spoke up now for the first time since their arrival. "You must forgive my dear friend, the Chef," he said, addressing José. "It's not the *chilaquiles* he finds fault with, it's the Chávez family."

"Why?" asked Trino. "What's wrong with them?"

"Señor Chávez," answered the soldier, "is a federal agent."

20

The Tent of the Two Generals

"And you mean to tell me that they fed you, stabled your horse, gave you a place to sleep, and sent you on your way, knowing all the while that you were on your way to *us*?"

"Yes, general sir, that's what I said. I told Señor Chávez that we wanted to find the Cristeros. He was so kind, and his wife made such—"

"I don't want to hear about her cooking, my young—what's your name again?"

"José—José Sánchez del Río."

"Yes, José, what amazes me is that they didn't tie you and your friend up right there and send you to México City. I just don't understand."

After dinner the night before, the boys had slept like logs until Private Mijares had awakened them, given them breakfast, and marched them over to headquarters.

Ever since he entered, José had been stealing glances about the large tent. In the center stood a small desk covered with maps and papers. Behind it sat two men, who introduced themselves as General Prudencio Mendoza and General Rubén Morfín. Piles of ammunition lined the side walls. In the back, long red sticks stacked one atop another formed a three foot wall. *Dynamite,* thought José.

All through General Prudencio's interrogation, General Morfín sat to the side fiddling with a pair of binoculars which dangled from his neck. Now he spoke.

"Perhaps Señor Chávez didn't think two boys could do much to help our cause," he hazarded.

"Good point, Morfín," said General Prudencio. Shifting his large frame once again toward José and Trino, he fixed them with a stare. Holding them in his gaze, he drew a monocle from the front pocket of his shirt and placed it on his left eye.

"And why, might I ask, did you two come all this way?"

José took a deep breath and stared the general back in the eyes. "We want to be Cristeros, and fight for Christ the King."

"And at your age, how do you exactly," he paused, fingering his monocle, "propose to do that?"

"I know I'm too young to use a rifle, but I can help in other ways. I know how to take care of horses, I can oil rifles, I can cook—"

General Prudencio's gaze had begun to wander off in the distance. General Morfín seemed to be cleaning his binoculars. A thought jumped into José's head. *Oh yeah, why didn't I tell them before?*

"—and I can play trumpet," he finished.

At this, General Morfín let his binoculars fall.

"Prudencio," he said, "That reminds me. You heard about Jorge, didn't you?"

"You mean your bugler?"

"Right. He could use a helper. None of the other men can squeeze a noise out of that blasted horn. And come to think of it, the flag bearer—"

"I see, I see, Morfín. If you need the boy, you can take him, just do me one favor—keep him away from the fighting."

"That can be arranged" he said, turning around. "The name's Morfín, General Morfín, and you?"

"I'm José Sánchez del Río," said the boy, breathing a sigh of relief.

"Well José, you'll be coming with me," said the general. "What about the other one?" he asked, turning to face General Prudencio, who was now twirling the monocle between his fingers.

The general sat up and slipped the eyepiece back between his cheek and eyebrow, fixing Trino with a stare.

"You said your name was—"

"Trino, short for José Trinidad Flores Espinosa."

"Very well, Trino," continued the general. "What do you have to say for yourself?"

Trino raised his head.

"I want to fight with the Cristeros too. I'll do anything you need me to. I'm ready to help."

"And he's a pretty good shot," added José.

Trino smiled.

"Hmm," said General Prudencio. "What do you say, Morfín?"

"Those federales already had their opportunity to capture you two," he said, looking from boy to boy. "Unless you go seeking for it, I doubt they'll get another chance."

He's awful short for a general, thought José, plodding along beside his new chief.

As they wound their way through the clusters of tents, group after group of soldiers stood and saluted. José noticed that many of their eyes weren't turned toward the general, but to him and Trino.

"My army is stationed over there," said General Morfín, pointing ahead to one of the large circles of tents.

"Do you always travel with General Prudencio?" asked José.

"Not always," answered Morfín. "In fact, we arrived yesterday and I'm planning on moving north next week. We try to stay on the move to keep the federals guessing."

"What about Chef Gustavo? Does he travel with you?" questioned Trino.

"No, though I wish he did. Chef Gustavo is General Prudencio's cook. We make do without him, though it is nice to have a decent meal now and then."

They pulled up outside a little brown tent.

"Let me think," said the general. "We need to find you a place to stay. José, you'll be close to my tent. Trino, I'll put you with Lieutenant Gódinez."

"OK," said Trino. "Do I get a rifle?"

"We'll see, we'll see."

"Um, General Morfín?" asked José, sheepishly.

"Yes son?"

"I was thinking that if the federals find out I've joined the Cristeros, they might try to punish my family."

"Well, yes, that's possible," answered the general, eyeing José. "It's part of the risk."

"Do you think… well, could I have a battle name—you know, one that wouldn't reveal my identity?"

"Hmmm. Not so bad an idea," said the general, sliding his hand up and down the strap of his binoculars. "A name that's different enough to confuse them, but not so different that it confuses us."

"How about Cuauhtémoc?" said Trino with a giggle.

"No," said General Morfín. "Let's keep it simple. José, from now on, your battle name will be *José Luis*."

21

Rusty Rifles

"Gosh, Trino, I can't feel my hand anymore. That must have been the eight-thousandth potato. How am I supposed to ride a horse now?"

"And how am I supposed to fire a gun? My hand feels like a *burro* stepped on it."

"Looks like you've been peeling *it* instead of the potatoes."

"Why can't they just eat the whole thing—skin and all?"

"Next time Chef Gustavo sticks his head in here, let's interrogate him."

"Better yet," said Trino, "let's hypnotize him and make him do the peeling."

"Yeah, good idea. You hypnotize him and I'll supply him with potatoes."

About their feet lay heaps of peels. Several pots sat around, filled with the fruit of their labors.

Trino looked up from his work. "Someone's coming," he said.

The canvas tent flap moved and light poured through. In stepped Private Mijares, still limping.

"And how are my young Cristeros getting along?" he asked, stopping just short of the mountain of potato peels.

"Half-dead," said Trino.

"Not dead yet, but getting there," added José.

Mijares glanced at his watch. "I left you with the generals three hours ago, and you already want to call it quits?"

"No," said José in a huff. "I didn't say anything about quitting."

"Good, good," replied the Private, gingerly prodding one of the piles with the toe of his boot. "I've come to rescue you from the clutches of Chef Gustavo. Clean up here, then meet me in the munitions tent."

"Yes sir," said José, jumping to his feet.

"Guess we don't have to hypnotize anybody after all," called Trino, running after José.

Trino slowly rubbed the rusty barrel of an old rifle with an oily cloth. "Guns are more exciting than potatoes… guns are more exciting than p…" he jerked himself awake with a start.

"But I can only take so much," said Trino, setting down the rusty old rifle.

"Don't do that," yawned José, as he squirted a drop of oil onto a knob and then started working it back and forth with his finger.

"So much cleaning—and no firing," Trino replied sleepily. "I want to see these things work."

"I just want to see if I can hit anything," said José.

"That's not hard. You just wait till you're calm, take aim, breathe out, and squeeze."

"Calm," said José, rubbing a rag up and down the long barrel of a Mauser. "That's the problem. How can you be calm in the middle of a battle?"

"I don't know," replied Trino, turning back to his work. "Guess I'll have to wait till the real thing to find out."

Later that night, flames leaped high into the air from a mammoth pile of wood. Rings of soldiers sat, cross-legged, all about.

Grasping his rosary between weary fingers, José got to his feet. "The third Joyful mystery," he announced, "is the birth of baby Jesus in Bethlehem."

As he finished the first half of the Hail Mary, his eyes swept around the circle.

It feels so different, he thought, as he waited for the soldiers to finish their part. *I'm praying about the first Christmas with Mary and Joseph and Baby Jesus, and here I am so far from home—like them.*

"Hail Mary, full of grace, the Lord is with thee…." he continued. "And blessed is the fruit of thy womb, Jesus."

After the rosary, the soldiers broke into groups and slowly made their way back to where they slept, some in tents, others in the open.

As José gazed up at the stars from beneath his blanket, it dawned on him: *I may be far from home, but this is where I belong, just like baby Jesus belonged in Bethlehem that first Christmas night. I'm sure he's happy to see me here, fighting for him.*

He pulled the blanket over his head and sleep overtook him.

22

Bugler

"Huh...? Go away."

"Get up, sleepy-head. It's time to wake this army."

José pulled the blanket away from his head and slowly pried an eyelid open. The sky was still black and ablaze with stars.

"Come on, son," said the soldier who had woken José up. You've got to play that little horn of yours for us."

"One second... let me get my shoes on."

As he slipped on his boots, thoughts came flickering through his head. The last three weeks with the Cristeros seemed like a blur of more odd jobs than he could remember. He had scrubbed pots and dishes, cleaned and oiled countless rifles, helped Chef Gustavo cook beans and tortillas, taken care of horses, carried water back and forth, minded the big campfire, helped soldiers take off their spurs, cleaned boots, served coffee, and run all kinds of errands.

After ten days General Morfín called José to his tent for the first time since they met. "Two things," the general told him. "First, I want you to be my bugler. That means you have to learn the calls. Second, I want you to be my flag bearer. Whenever we're on the move, you don't leave my side."

José had spent the rest of the day nearly jumping from place to place he was so excited.

"The problem with being bugler during war," explained Jorge, the head bugler, "is that you can't practice. Any noise you make, the men assume it's a command. So every chance you get to play for real you have to use as practice—there's no better way to learn bugle."

After he had crawled out of bed and slipped his shoes on, José began to blast off the shrill notes on his little horn. Grunts and yawns poured from the sleeping forms on the ground and from inside the tents. Some soldiers didn't stir until their companions gave them a jab in the side. Others jumped up quickly and tidied themselves and their sleeping areas.

After ten minutes, all of the men had assembled in front of General Morfín's tent. Morfín stepped out, binoculars dangling from his neck.

"Kneel down, soldiers of Christ the King." he said.

Everyone, oldest to youngest—even the general himself—knelt on the dusty ground to offer their day to God.

It's kind of like morning prayers at home, thought José. *Only there's a lot more of us.*

Later that morning, a new boy strode into camp. He came across José and Trino as they hovered around a large wooden box.

"What are you doing?" asked the boy.

Trino paused in the middle of folding a piece of white cloth. José held a large red book in his hand.

"Straightening up after Mass," answered Trino, looking up at the newcomer. The boy was short and had dark skin and the flat face of an Indian.

"What's your name?" Trino asked.

"I'm Lorenzo," he answered. "I'm General Prudencio's new message boy."

"Welcome to the Cristeros," said José, smiling. "I'm José Luis, and this is Trino." The boys shook hands.

"Do you always have Mass?" asked Lorenzo peering into the open box.

"No," answered José. "Just when there's a priest here."

"Who said Mass today?"

"Padre Tomás," answered Trino, "but he just left for another camp."

"Does he say Mass out here in the open?"

"Sí," Trino replied. "We built a small portable altar, and the soldiers assemble there with their rifles and flags and all. José and I get to serve. It's great, especially when padre gives communion to all the men.

"As a Cristero," added José, "every time you receive communion, you know it could be your last."

That afternoon, José reported for duty. General Morfín was studying some papers strewn across his desk.

"Where's your horse?" asked the general as José walked in.

"Oh, Copper? He's tied up with the others."

"Well José—*José Luis*—you'd better go saddle him up. We ride in ten minutes."

23

Why We Fight

José hurried down the path toward the horses, flag in hand. Most of the other men had already left. A few stragglers were adjusting their saddles and cantering off.

Copper's ears gave a twitch as José called his name. The boy leaned the flag against a fence and struggled to lift his saddle into place. His trembling fingers didn't seem to remember how to fasten the buckles.

He paused with bridle in hand.

"We can do this, right boy? This is what we came here for." He leaned his head against the horse's neck. Copper whinnied and stamped a foot.

After slipping the bit between the animal's teeth José buckled the bridle straps and climbed into the saddle.

Grabbing the flag, he gave a flick on the reins, Copper started off.

General Morfín was waiting by his tent. He sat atop what looked like a mustang—white and brown with flecks of black.

"Ready?" he asked, setting off at a trot.

"Yes sir!" replied José, following the general's lead.

"I want you to stay close by me and out of trouble," said Morfín as they trotted along. "The men look to the flag for assurance. If you go down, it spells disaster. Understand?"

José nodded.

"Do you remember your bugle calls?"

"Yes sir, general sir," José replied.

By now the two had reached a clearing where the other soldiers waited atop their horses.

The general rode through the center of his troops, and then paused a second to talk with his aides before trotting off.

The mass of men started forward ever so slowly behind their general. José glanced up at the flag in his hands. It was green, white, and red, with *"Viva Cristo Rey y Nuestra Señora de Guadalupe"* written on it. Emblazoned in the center was Our Lady of Guadalupe.

As they drew near the forest, José kept his eyes on General Morfín. The general's mustang started to pick up speed.

Tucking the flag against his side, José lowered his head below the branches whipping past. The reins trailed limp in his hands.

Copper was following close upon the heels of Morfín's horse. Both animals raced down the hillside.

José peeked to his right and noticed another horse galloping alongside them.

These Cristeros are crazy, he thought.

After several minutes of plunging down the hill and through the forest, an open patch came into view ahead. Soon they were speeding across a field of grass and small bushes.

José unfurled the flag. Wind tore at it, dragging the pole backwards.

"You take care of directions, Copper," he hollered, "and I'll take care of the flag." The horse seemed to like this plan, for with an extra burst of speed he pulled even with General Morfín's mustang.

Now they were riding down the side of a valley between two mountain ranges. The scrub brush gave way to flat ground.

To his left, José saw a small cluster of houses sitting on the grassy plain. Farther ahead lay another, bigger group.

Once past the houses, General Morfín slowed to a trot. As the other riders started to bunch up behind, he pulled his horse to a halt.

Binoculars to his eyes, he gazed back and forth along the horizon.

José looked in the same direction, but all he could see were the bushes near at hand, and the hills far away.

Before long, the other Cristeros arrived on the scene. Soon they formed a huge semicircle with General Morfín in the center. By his side, José sat atop Copper, flag unfurled in his hand.

"Men," spoke General Morfín after the last horse had pulled to a stop, "our scouts tell me that a group of federal soldiers from Quitupan are on patrol south of Cotija."

Yesterday they started a slow movement in our direction, and they should be nearing the hills in the middle of the valley soon. Now I know it will be dark soon, but we'll have the element of surprise. If we get there before them and manage to take the high ground, I believe we can inflict heavy casualties. It might make them rethink their offensive entirely. My hope is that we can do this without losing any of our men."

"I want to be sure you men know why we fight."

All eyes were fixed on him now.

"We aren't vigilantes out to cause trouble. Nor are we fighting for just a man, or even for a group of men. This army is different." The general let his gaze drift from face to face.

"I know why I'm here – to fight the unjust oppression of our present government, and restore freedom of worship to our people. I'd rather achieve this without war, but war is our only choice.

"You who fight with me," continued Morfín, extending his hand, "I hope you understand this. Never forget why we fight. Whatever happens today, or any other day, we will not stop until they give us back our churches... or we all die fighting."

Morfín swallowed. "Any man who doesn't want this is free to leave right now. We'll ask no questions, and hold no grudges."

The soldiers shuffled in their saddles and looked around at their companions. José gripped the flag, his heart beating wildly. The general waited a moment in silence, then nodded.

"Stay by my side, boy," he whispered to José.

Raising his rifle high in the air, he shouted, *"Bien. Vámonos. Viva Cristo Rey!"*

"Viva Cristo Rey, y Viva la Vírgen de Guadalupe!" the men shouted back, raising their rifles high.

24

The Battle of Los Cutos

Wind lashed at José's hair. A smile shone across his face. This was just how he had imagined life in the Cristeros would be.

He thought back to last week, when General Morfín had given him his own rifle.

"Yours to have, not to use, unless there's grave need," the general had told him.

After descending from the mountains, the army moved slowly. General Morfín wended his way through shaded valleys and hollows, attempting to mask his troops' movements from unfriendly eyes.

He was astute, this little man with binoculars. He planned all his attacks meticulously, for never once did he hesitate, or pause to study a map. Half an hour after they had left their rallying point, he had his troops lined up at the foot of a small grassy hill. All was quiet.

The hill rose above them about 200 feet. Its sides were mainly open, with a few trees and bushes scattered about.

Movement in some tall grass at the base of the hill caught José's attention.

"*Que hay*, Pato?" asked General Morfín.

The grass stopped moving and a man pulled himself up from the ground. He ambled over to the general and saluted.

"Not twenty minutes ago they were about three miles off, headed straight this way, *mi general*. They should be in position soon."

"I wish I could see through this hill right now," muttered the general. "What about their numbers?"

"Well sir," replied the scout, "I didn't have the best observation post. But there is at least a battalion."

General Morfín played with his binoculars.

"With all due respect, sir, I think that now is the moment," continued the scout. "They wouldn't expect us to attack them out here in the open, and especially this late in the day."

"I see what you mean," replied Morfín. His eyebrows were gathered into furrows and his eyes closed shut for a moment.

No one moved.

"Alright men, the sun's almost down – so we have little time. There will be three movements. The first time you hear the bugle, that's for Camacho on the left. You'll show yourselves but then take up defensive positions. The second blast is for Attila in the front. You'll charge down the hill. Villa, the third blast is for you and your men. You'll circle *los federales* and take them from behind."

The men nodded.

"Alright, Villa, you first," said the general, motioning.

A group of soldiers started off to the right.

"Camacho, you're next."

Another group of men set off around the left side of the hill.

"Your turn, Attila, and stay low up top. Wait for my signal."

This last group of soldiers started up the center of the hill. General Morfín followed them, a little back and to the left.

José took the rear. Sweat began to line his palms as he gripped the flag.

The hill was an easy climb for the horses. Just below the summit, General Morfín dismounted and gave his reins to José. Then he slowly walked the little distance that remained to the top.

José glanced to his right and saw the soldiers loading their rifles. His eyes strayed down to his own weapon. It was a bit rusty in places, and the barrel had a few long scratches. *Hope I don't have to use this thing,* he thought.

Seconds later, a low whistle caught his attention. General Morfín was waving from the top of the hill.

The general held his hand up, palm toward José. Then he began a countdown with his fingers.

The bugle—where was it? Hanging from his neck. But he only had two hands. Hoping the general's horse would stay put, José released the reins and scrambled for his instrument. As he lifted the mouthpiece to his lips, he racked his brain to remember the notes for "Charge."

The general dropped the last of his fingers just as José realized in horror that he had forgotten the call. To make matters worse, the mustang at his side, now conscious of its freedom, started up the hill. Morfín waved his arms in frustration.

One long, drawn-out blast spilled from the bugle.

"Better than nothing," said José, letting the instrument fall from his lips.

To José's joy, the stray mustang had made straight for General Morfín. The boy dismounted and walked Copper up the rest of the hill. On reaching the summit, he let out a sigh. The troops had understood. Cristero soldiers were streaming out from the left.

Down on the plain, a serpentine mass of grey was weaving its way toward them between the small hills.

"Sorry about the bugle," said José.

"Forget about it," answered Morfín, still glued to his binoculars. "I'm worried about *los federales*—there's more than I thought. You remember the notes for 'Retreat' don't you?"

"*Sí, mí general.*"

"Good. We might need it. But first, I'm going to send Attila and his men down there. You be ready with your bugle."

As José and General Morfín watched in the fading light, the two Cristero columns made their way through the brush and over the small hills that separated them from the federals in grey.

Camacho's soldiers on the left began taking positions behind boulders and bushes. On the right, Villa and his men made for the rear of the federal troops. Camacho was the bait; Villa the trap.

"Now. Signal another charge."

José put the bugle to his lips and blew with all his might. Springing up from where they had been hiding to his left, Attila's men came pouring over the top of the hill and into view of the approaching federals.

"Good, that scared them," said General Morfín, surveying the action below. "We might do some damage yet."

The body of federal troops had now halted in the narrow valley.

To the left, Camacho's soldiers began to rush out against the federal flank. With Attila and his men pouring down the hill front, the federals started to pull back.

"Look at the fools," said General Morfín, gazing out through his binoculars. "They're spread out as thin as a teaspoon of Tequila on a frying pan."

As José watched from beside Copper, the federal troops continued to pull back. "They're retreating, aren't they?" he asked.

General Morfín seemed not to hear. Through his binoculars he scanned the horizon apprehensively. "Getting dark fast," he murmured. "We'd better finish this up soon. José, blow that horn of yours again. It's time for Villa to take them from behind."

José raised the gleaming instrument to his lips and blasted out the familiar notes once again.

Far out upon the plain, a dark blur streamed out from the right.

"They're supposed to hit from behind, not from the side!" fumed Morfín. "What's gotten into their heads this time?"

The Cristero soldiers under Villa had collided with the federal troops about two thirds of the way down their main column. From where Jose and the general stood, all they could here were the shouts of the men and bullets firing.

"Looks like this could turn into a bloodbath," said Morfín despondently. "Call them off."

José turned to the general and hesitated.

"Come on boy, you heard what I said. Take that blasted horn of yours and sound retreat!"

This time José remembered the notes.

"Well now," said the general, surveying the scene below. "Let's see if our men can make it back safe in the darkness."

"You should have seen their faces when we poured out from behind that hill."

"Sí, their general was right there, next to his horse, and he took off running. Salcido got the horse *and* the general's sword."

"Was it that white horse you brought back?"

"That's the one, a real beauty."

The bonfire burned bright and tall amid the circle of seated men. The Cristeros had made it back to their camp safely, and once there, the day's battle had been all they talked about.

"We gave the captured horse to General Morfín. He called it '*un caballo noble*'," said one of the men to his companion.

"We'll need to do more than just steal horses and swords if we want to win this war," said a third man. "We didn't take any hostages, and there weren't any casualties either."

"That was because it was already dark," said the first man. "Give us some daylight, and we'll finish that army off."

And blessed is the fruit of thy womb, Jesus." José led the men in a rosary of thanksgiving for the successful operation.

On the opposite side of the circle, a grizzled soldier sat with his legs crossed, cigarette dangling from his lip.

"Look at him," he said, giving his friend a kick.

"What?" replied the man, stirring from his nap.

"Reminds me of Saint Tarcisius, he does, leading us all like that."

"You mean little José Luis?"

"Thirteen, and he's already a Cristero."

"I sure hope he lasts. In my book, boys his age only make easy targets for federal bullets," said the second man matter-of-factly.

"That," said the old soldier, slowly snuffing out his cigarette, "is why he reminds me of Tarcisius."

25

Nervous Horse

A whinny came from behind the clump of trees.

It was two days later, and row upon row of rifles gleamed in the morning sunlight. Padre Tomás had arrived the night before, and now he was celebrating Mass for the troops at a portable altar.

"*Dominus vobiscum,*" said the priest in a low voice.

"*Et cum spiritu tuo,*" replied José, hands folded.

The horse neighed again.

"Isn't that General Morfín's new horse?" asked José, whispering.

"Sí," replied Trino, who stood by his side, "*pero que pasa?*"

The animal started pulling at its rope. Now the other horses started to stir as well.

Meanwhile, the men seemed oblivious. Most of them knelt on the ground, praying.

José's eye caught movement off in the distance. *What's that?* he thought, gazing out over the heads of the Cristeros. He saw metal glinting in the sun.

"Someone's coming!" he shouted.

Instantly, a hundred heads turned and stared in José's direction. For a moment, he felt like a fool, then he pointed a trembling hand toward the north.

"Los federales!" shouted a voice. The phrase was taken up and repeated, "Los federales, los federales!"

The troops had gotten to their feet now the shouting grew furious.

Some of the men had already laid down in the grass to take up positions. They trained their rifles in the direction of the attackers.

"We don't have bullets!" said a voice. "We can't fight like this!"

"*Cállate*!" cried another voice. It was General Morfín, binoculars in hand.

"Men, this valley is no place to fight," he shouted. "I want you to separate, find ammunition, and regroup on the ridge." He pointed to the line of peaks behind him. The men held their silence.

"Now! Let's move it!" shouted the general.

As the men headed off, José tugged on the long white vestment Father Tomás was wearing. "Padre, what do we do about the things for Mass?"

"*No te preocupes, niño,*" said the priest, clearing the altar. "We'll take the important things with us – here, you help with the ciborium, and Trino, you take the Missal – and we'll leave the altar."

"Padre, let's go," shouted a Cristero soldier.

The small group started into the forest just as the first of the federal soldiers came into sight.

It could have been a lot worse," said Padre Tomás.

"Sí," added Trino, "If it weren't for José Luis, we could have all been captured."

"It wasn't me," protested José, walking along beside the other two, "the general's horse gave the alarm."

"You *and* the general's horse," corrected Padre Tomás.

The federal troops hadn't pressed their luck when they found the Cristeros gone. After grabbing everything of value they headed off again. The two boys and the priest were looking over the scene of the day's raid.

"What about the portable altar?" asked José. "Why would they want that?"

"No sé," replied the padre. "We'll have to find something to take its place. I'm just glad that's the biggest thing they captured."

26

Picazo's Plan

In his corner office, Rafael Picazo listened to the federal General explain the day's events.

"We reached their camp, but somehow they knew beforehand that we were coming."

"You're not impressing me, General Tranquilino. We can't win this war through evading real battles."

"That's true, Rafael, but if we keep hoping that they'll come and fight us in the open, this war will last another hundred years."

"Look general, I really don't care exactly what you do. The way I see it, we have to take out their leadership. Cut off the head," here he sliced his hand through the air, "and the body shrivels up."

"Rafael, let me get this straight: you're asking me to change the whole objective of this mission?"

The Mayor pulled the cigar from between his teeth, leaned forward, and whispered, "What do you think the President will say when he receives the telegram announcing you've captured a Cristero general?"

Stepping back, General Tranquilino's right hand wandered up to the rows of medals and pins on his chest.

"How do you suppose I go about capturing a general?"

Picazo made his way over to the window that looked out on the town square. His reflection stared him back. Adjusting his moustache, he spoke. "Only a general knows another general's games. Where are you at your most vulnerable? How could they capture you? Think up a plan—I'm sure you'll do fine."

General Tranquilino nodded his head. "I'll figure something out, I'm sure. We ride in half an hour."

"Good. I'll be waiting for news of the capture. There's plenty of space in my jail."

José gazed at the scenery as he rode along. Flowers were blooming in all the trees they passed. "Spring is already here," he thought. "I can't wait until we can have fresh fruit again."

He pulled his horse level with the general's mustang. "Any orders, sir?" he asked.

"Nothing special today," said General Morfín, sauntering along, "just a few telephone lines to cut south of Cotija."

"Yes sir," replied José, bouncing along atop Copper.

After the surprise attack during Mass, the Cristeros had changed camp and laid low for several days. One of the women who brought them food had given José a letter from his parents. In it they told him of their plans to move to Guadalajara for the rest of the war. Things were becoming too dangerous in Sahuayo.

"General Morfín?"

"Yes José Luis?"

"How did the federal soldiers know where our camp was?"

The General shook his head. "*Ni idea,*" he said.

"What if they're still following us?" asked the boy.

"Then God save us."

"Are you sure the Cristero scum will pass by here?" demanded the soldier. His grey uniform matched the column of men stretching behind him into the woods. They stood in the shade of the trees lining a long, narrow valley. The valley itself was open grassland, and the trees provided excellent cover.

"Sí, señor," replied the peasant, "this is the only way."

"If you're wrong, you'll regret it," growled the soldier, pushing the man away. He turned to the group of men.

"Spread out along the tree line here, and take cover," he said. "We attack when I give the word. Remember," he stated emphatically waving his fist, "we want General Morfín alive."

"How much farther?" demanded General Morfín.

"This hut is about half way down the valley," said the scout, pointing to a little brick structure on their left. "We'll reach the plains in five minutes. The telephone lines are right there."

"Should be easy, right?" asked the general, bouncing up and down on his white horse.

"If your men are ready," replied the scout.

José rode along atop Copper. *Seems simple enough,* he thought to himself. *But I still can't wait till we're over with this job.*

Just then, a loud crack came from the woods. General Morfín's white horse reared up and then fell backwards.

"It's an ambush!" shouted the scout, turning his horse and galloping off.

"Good shot."

"What about the other horse, the one with the boy?"

"Let it go, the boy will bolt. We want the old man."

"What if they both ride off?"

"They won't get far on one horse."

"Alright."

"OK men, keep your weapons out. Morfín's too smart to fight all of us, but he might try something fast. Whatever happens, we take him alive. Let's move."

"My horse—where, how...?" gasped General Morfín.

Blood poured from his horse's side, and the animal struggled weakly.

"Up by the trees, look," said José, who had pulled to a halt beside where the general lay sprawled in the grass.

Morfín scrambled to his feet and stared. Bullets whizzed around them, and below them on the plane the Cristero line was already fragmented. "José, flee, now," he said, still trying to catch his breath from the fall.

"Mi General, no!"

"It's a trap. Go—now! I'll be ok."

José watched the figures in grey pouring out of the trees from behind the hut. The Cristero soldiers were fleeing in all directions. He turned to General Morfín and shook his head. *"Mí general, aquí está mi caballo"* said the boy, jumping off Copper and holding out the reins. "You take my horse."

Morfín, shook his head and pointed. *"Muchacho! Corre! Vete!* Are you mad? Fly, now!"

"Look, general, take my horse and save yourself. You're more necessary for the cause than me. I'll be ok."

General Morfín glanced at the advancing troops again. The federal soldiers were only seconds away.

"God be with you, son," said Morfín, gently laying a hand on José's shoulder.

Putting a foot in the stirrups, the general quickly swung himself up onto Copper. José touched the horse's side just as Morfín flicked the reins.

A lone figure stood in the valley.

"There goes the boy," announced one of the soldiers as they galloped along.

"Good. Just one old man left now."

"Hey, who gets the reward for all this?"

"Mind your own business. You'll get paid."

"But—"

BANG! A loud explosion came from the valley's bottom and a bullet hissed past their heads.

"Everyone find cover, now!"

The federal soldiers spurred their horses to the small brick farmhouse on their right.

Once in its shadow, they dismounted.

"You should have let me shoot him."

"Quiet! He isn't worth anything dead."

"Neither are we!"

"You don't look dead yet. Listen to me. You four spread out and come from behind. I'll take the center. All we have to do is grab him."

"Just give me one shot, and he's ours."

"No way. You heard me. We're taking him alive."

In the hollow of the valley, José's fingers trembled as he tried to pull back the bolt on his rifle. The dead horse felt warm against his side. In his hand, the bullet didn't want to fit into the hot firing chamber. When at last the chamber opened, the cartridge slipped from his hand and fell to the ground.

"Why didn't I practice more?" he asked himself, managing to slide another bullet into place.

Turning, he peeked over the horse's belly. "What?" he exclaimed.

Only one figure remained where before there had been five.

He scanned to the left and right—nothing—just one man, approaching slowly. A heavy silence filled the valley. Leaning his weapon across the horse's belly, José trained it on the lone figure in grey. The sweaty palm of his index finger touched the cold metal trigger. He squeezed.

27

Prisoners

The door swung open and blinding sunlight sliced through the darkness. A vague outline materialized in the doorway. Someone gasped, and then there came a thump. All was still.

Except the crying.

"*Que pasa*?"

"Who's that?" said a high voice, inhaling quickly.

"Wait a minute, you sound familiar. Is that you, Lorenzo?

"José?" asked the high voice.

"*Híjole*! Lorenzo, am I glad to see you."

José walked over to his little friend and helped him to his feet. "How did you end up here?" he asked, grabbing the boy by the shoulders. "You should be with General Prudencio, shouldn't you?"

"They caught me. The General had asked me to deliver a message to General Morfín..."

"That's my General."

"...and they stopped me. Asked me what I was up to. I told them I was looking for something to eat, which was the truth. But they searched me and found the letter. Then they brought me here."

As he finished his story, both boys sat down and leaned their backs against the wall.

"What about you, José—what happened to you?"

"Well, I was with General Morfín and we were going to cut some telephone lines. Then his horse got shot. It was a trap. So I gave him my horse. Then I covered his escape. I was just about to shoot one of the federals, when a big fellow jumped on me from behind and pinned me to the ground. When they realized that I wasn't the General, they went crazy. They kicked me and hit me and tossed me around. Four of them aimed their rifles right at me, and I thought I was *muerto*. But the fifth one screamed at them and grabbed me. He tied my hands and put a rope around my neck, and then threw me in this hut."

"What will they do with us?" asked Lorenzo.

"*Ni idea,*" replied José. "Maybe just send us home. I'm from Sahuayo. What about you?"

"Me?—I'm from Jiquilpan."

"That's close to Sahuayo. I had to pass by it on my way to join the Cristeros."

"Well I've never been to Sahuayo. I sure hope they send me back home."

"I hope so too, Lorenzo."

In his office, Rafael Picazo crumpled the paper in the palm of his hand and squeezed. Then, snatching the cigar from his mouth he screamed in frustration.

"*Tontos*—can't even catch a miserable Cristero general!" he stamped excitedly, waving his arms. "What good is some boy to me?"

In the corner, by the door, the messenger in grey trembled. "I wasn't in the battle sir—"

"I didn't ask your opinion," broke in Picazo, fingering his moustache. "Give me some paper."

Dipping his pen in the inkstand, Picazo hesitated. "Do I want this boy?" he wondered aloud.

The messenger didn't move.

"I asked you a question," said Picazo between clenched teeth.

"Sí *señor. No señor. Ahh… No sé.*"

Picazo was now nodding his head. "So that's what you think, is it?"

"Sí *señor.*"

"Good thing you're just delivering messages."

Popping his cigar back into place, Picazo took the pen and held it over the paper.

Tranquilino–

Disappointed.

Think up new plan.
Send boy to me.
Both boys. I'll take
care of them.

—Picazo

28

Dear Mom

Cotija Mich. February Monday 6 of 1928

Señora María del Río de Sanchez.
Guadalajara. Jal.

My dear Mamá,

I was taken prisoner in battle today. I think that soon I will die, but that doesn't matter Mamá. Please accept the will of God – I die very happy, because I die in battle alongside our Lord. Don't you worry about me dying; your worrying is what would be hardest for me. Just tell my brothers and sisters to follow their littlest brother's example, and do the will of God. Take courage, and send me your blessing along with Papá's.

Say goodbye to everyone for me one last time, and finally, may you receive the heart of your son who loves you so dearly and wants to see you so much before he dies.

José Sanchez del Río.

"Better prepare her for the worst, right Lorenzo?" said José, folding the letter up.

Lorenzo shifted as he sat. "José, does it hurt to die?"

José gulped. "I don't know. I hope it's quick."

Lorenzo nervously rubbed his knee. "José, are we going to die?"

Setting down his pen and paper and slowly exhaling, José shut his eyes. Leaning forward, he cradled his head between his two hands.

"*No sé,* Lorenzo. I really don't know."

Outside the little hut, two men debated.

"One horse."

"You sure?"

"Just do what I say, private. If they refuse my offer, we're sending them straight to Picazo."

"Yes sir, General Tranquilino."

"Good. And tie their hands nice and stiff. Wouldn't want the only captives we have to escape now, would we?"

The two men stopped in front of the knotty wooden door.

"*Ábrela.*"

Private Gómez inserted a key and undid the padlock hanging from a bar across the door. Setting this aside, he gave a tug and heaved it open.

"*Buenos días prisioneros.* How are we doing this morning?"

The two boys were sprawled out next to each other asleep on the floor. First one, then the other, lifted his head and looked around.

"Yes, you are prisoners, if you remember," said General Tranquilino.

"And who are you?" asked José shielding his eyes from the glare.

"If you knew anything about an army," said the General, "you'd be able to tell from my medals."

He looked his captives up and down.

"Gómez," he whispered, "You sure these are the right ones?"

"What do you mean sir?" asked the private, puzzled.

"They don't look like soldiers to me," replied the general.

Private Gómez made as if to speak, but General Tranquilino held up a hand.

"You boys don't know what you've gotten yourselves into. Bad things are in store for you. We—" he hesitated, "—get rid of all the Cristeros we capture."

He paused to see the boys' reactions.

José scratched the short black hair on his head. Lorenzo rubbed his eyes.

The general continued. "But me—I'm a nice fellow. I've decided to forgive you."

The boys perked up, really listening now.

"All you have to do…" he paused.

José and Lorenzo had now risen to their feet. "Is what?" José asked hopefully.

"All you have to do," he continued, "is join our side."

Both José and Lorenzo frowned.

"Look boys, you've been fighting for the wrong side. The Cristero army is illegitimate, unofficial, and destined for failure. We federals stand for law and order. We stand for peace. You have fought against the legitimate government of your country and you deserve to die. But I'll forgive you right here and now – let you walk free – as long as you join our side."

The general folded his arms across his chest and looked from boy to boy.

José rubbed a hand through his black, disheveled hair.

"Was it 'law and order' that murdered Anacleto Gonzalez Flores?" he asked. "Was it law and order that came into our town and took over our churches? Was it law and order that shot my uncle, Padre Ignacio?"

"You don't know what you're talking about son, those are all complicated situations," replied the general.

"Freedom to go to Church doesn't seem that complicated to me," José replied.

"You want me to join you side?" the boy continued, clenching his fists. "Well here's my answer: I'll never join the side of the persecutors of the Church. I'd rather die. I'm your enemy. Shoot me!"

29

Destination Unknown

"José, where are they taking us?" asked Lorenzo, his little frame jolting back and forth atop the horse. The boys had been traveling for several hours now, blindfolded.

"*Ni idea,*" José replied. "I wonder how Copper's doing."

"Who's Copper—your dog?"

"My horse—the one that saved General Morfín's life."

"I'll bet he's better off than we are."

"Anything's better than having your hands tied, your eyes covered, and no idea where you're going."

"José, I don't get it," began Lorenzo.

"Qué?"

"You."

José was silent.

"What made you speak to the general like that? And what's going to happen to us now? He was furious with us, almost kicked that soldier. He took what you said as my answer too."

"What would you have said?" asked José, trying to use his tongue to lift the bandana away from his eyes. It stayed in place.

"Something different—something that wouldn't have gotten us into more trouble..."

"Lorenzo, I'm sorry," said José, as he heard his companion start to cry once more.

"Lorenzo?" asked José after they had gone along a while.

"Sí?" said the boy from between sniffles.

"It's not as bad as it seems."

"Why's that?"

"Prisoners aren't allowed to talk," broke in a voice, menacingly.

"I won't talk if you take off this bandana," ventured José.

"General's orders," replied the voice.

"Where's the general now?"

"*Cállate niño.* If you keep talking, you'll end up walking the rest of the way."

José and Lorenzo fell into an uneasy silence. From behind their blindfolds, all they could sense was which direction the sunlight was coming from. With their hands tied behind their backs, it was all they could do to hold on when their horse headed up or down hills and over dry stream beds.

One question nagged at José's mind: "Where are we going?"

The massive oak door lurched inward on its hinges. José held his breath.

"Welcome," said the soldier, pushing the two boys from behind. "Welcome to prison."

"No," whispered José, his voice dropping to a hush.

His face had lit up just moments earlier when the soldier had taken off their blindfolds. A quick glance around had revealed that they were standing in the atrium of his parish church, *Santiago,* in Sahuayo.

"This is *my* town," he had whispered to Lorenzo with pride.

Before his eyes could adjust to the darkness of the church, José had grown tense. The smell wafting up from the pews was not of incense, candles, or flowers. It was the smell of manure—fresh manure.

"Come on, this way," said the soldier giving a sharp tug on the rope. Lorenzo whimpered a little. The cord had been rubbing against his wrists all day, and now they were raw to the touch.

The soldier pulled them to the left. José wanted to tell him to watch out for the pews, but then he realized that there were no pews. Along the walls lay heaps of rubbish. A horse was nosing around in a pile of hay. At the foot of the altar smoldered a small fire. Odds and ends of what had been the pews lay scattered about. The statues in the niches behind the altar had all been reduced to stumps of plaster. It looked like someone had used them for target practice. Roosters wandered about, pecking at the ground.

The soldier led them along the back wall and into a small room with a vaulted roof. It was the baptistery. The large fresco of Jesus' Baptism on the back wall was still intact, though here and there was scribbled a profanity. In the center of the room stood the marble baptismal font. A grated window off to the side let in a few feeble rays of light.

"Aquí están," said the soldier, untying them. "Welcome to your new home."

Up in his corner office, Picazo listened to the messenger announce the boys' arrival.

"Bueno," he said, fumbling with his lighter. "I'll be down shortly."

"Sí señor," replied the soldier, turning on his heels and leaving the office.

"Caray," said Picazo to himself, as he gave the first puff on his cigar. "Don Macario can't seem to keep his brats out of trouble."

He sat down, and stared at the portrait of President Calles.

"Why did I ever have to become this kid's *padrino*?" he wondered aloud.

He looked again at the papers on his desk. The sentence for all rebel prisoners was death, and José had been caught red-handed. He shook his head.

"How can I please the President, and save Macario's boy?"

In Guadalajara, a small figure beat his fist against a door.

"Señor Sánchez. Señora Sánchez. It's me, Rafa, please open up," said a lanky boy banging on the door.

Don Macario Sánchez undid a series of locks and peered through the opening.

"Sorry I didn't answer your first knock, Rafa, it's just that—"

"I don't have long. I came to deliver some news. The Cristeros are saying that José was captured yesterday."

Don Macario swayed and grabbed for the doorframe. "Where is he? Is he injured?"

Rafa hunched his shoulders. "I'm not sure. They—they bring most prisoners to Sahuayo, but no one has seen José yet. There'll be more news soon, I'm sure. It's best if you just wait here."

"Wait?" asked Don Macario peering forward. "No. No I can't. I'll go find him." He started to close the door.

"But—but what about your family?" asked Rafa.

"They'll be safer here in Guadalajara."

30

Choices

After a whole day on horseback, neither boy had taken a seat in their new prison cell. Lorenzo was peering through the bars of the window into the street, while José examined the baptismal font.

A lone figure came striding through the church and into the baptistery. "On your feet, prisoners," barked the guard reflexively.

A frown spread across José's face.

Rafael Picazo stopped just feet away. "*Muchachos,*" he said, spreading his palms, "what are two young men like you doing in a place like this?"

Silence. The two boys only stared.

Picazo gave a long pull on his cigar and frowned.

"José, what have you been up to?"

José looked at his *padrino*, "I've been off with the men, fighting," he said.

Picazo gave another pull on his cigar and let out a long trail of smoke. "Fighting?" he asked. "That's not right. You should be in school, shouldn't you?" Without waiting for a response, he pulled a paper from his pocket. Lowering his voice, he took José by the shoulder and stepped aside.

"Look son, these are my orders. You were captured fighting for the rebels. You know the sentence for that."

José nodded.

"Now listen. I know they tricked you into this. Your father and I have been good friends since we were boys. I don't want to do what this paper says I have to do, for his sake," he paused, "and for yours."

He paused again to see what effect his words were having on the boy. José was listening.

Picazo dropped his voice to a hush. "Now, I've decided to put you on a train to Texas first thing tomorrow. You can wait out the war there. When things have calmed down here, we'll bring you back."

José stood in thought a little. He ran a hand through his short black hair.

"Señor Picazo…," he started.

"Yes son, go on."

"I…"

Before he could continue, memories and sounds started welling up before his mind's eye. A campfire, surrounded by soldiers, blazed in the night. The sound was of voices praying a rosary. Those same soldiers marched by day to battle. Then came a charge. All the while, an empty saddle floated before him. There was no bugler.

He hung his head, and then shook it. "No. No, I can't."

"*Qué?*" asked Picazo, tilting his head quizzically.

"Look Señor Picazo: if you let me go, I'll join up with the Cristeros to fight again."

Picazo's face went red. The veins on his neck began to bulge. Before speaking, he inhaled deeply.

"I know what you mean, son. Once you've had a taste of battle, you thrive on it. If you want to become a soldier, so be it. I know some of the finest military schools around. I'm sure I can find you a place. They'll teach you how to use all kinds of weapons. You'll learn strategy and tactics—you know—the art of war. You'll become a real soldier. In no time you could be an officer."

The smile mechanically plastered across Picazo's face began to twitch at the edges.

José's eyes glanced around at the filth lining the church, *his* church. From nearby in the sanctuary, a rooster crowed. Hooves sounded lightly on the tile floor.

Ever so carefully, he lifted his head until he stood level with Rafael Picazo's shoulders. Then he exhaled slowly. His lips were drawn taut in one fine line.

"I'd rather die. I joined the Cristeros to open up the churches again. I'll never fight for the persecutors of the Church."

Picazo gulped. His smile caved in. In its place, his face assumed a mask of steel.

"You know what this means, boy?"

The setting sun cast its last radiant colors across the sky. Shadows began to fill the baptistery.

Lorenzo sat in the corner, poking at his foot.

"*Qué pasa*?" asked José, tossing pebbles against the wall.

"It's just—I'm scared. What are they going to do with us?"

"I wish I knew. You heard my *padrino* this afternoon. He wants me to join his side and follow one of his crazy schemes."

"And why don't you?" Lorenzo broke in. "I mean, at least to get out of this prison. Once you're free, you can join the Cristeros again."

José shook his head. "No, Lorenzo. No, I can't. That would be denying everything I've been fighting for. I'd feel so hollow."

Lorenzo looked intently at José for a moment. "But what about me, José? I don't want to die."

"The truth is," sighed José, "neither do I."

31

Roosters in the Sanctuary

Rubbing his eyes, José sat up from where he had been sleeping. He let out a big yawn. Outside, the sun had not yet peeked above the horizon.

He needed to go to the bathroom—but where? Not here in the church. Getting to his feet he started forward.

As he stepped out of the baptistery and turned left, movements by the altar caught his attention. There, on top of the tabernacle, sat a large rooster, its bright red head clearly visible in the dim light.

José paused in his tracks. Feathers and muck crowned the top of the tabernacle, and long trails of green slime lined its sides.

To his right, another rooster sat on the altar. This too was covered in filth.

A third animal lay huddled, sleeping in a ball at the altar's foot.

"There where you belong, Lord, they tie up their fighting roosters. I won't stand for it," José whispered, shaking his head.

He slipped back into the baptistery, careful not to disturb his little friend sleeping in the corner. A minute's worth of rubbing the rope that bound his hands on one of the rusty metal bars in the window snapped the cord.

"José?" came a voice from the darkness.

"Sorry to have woken you up, Lorenzo."

"What are you up to?" the little boy asked.

"Someone tied his roosters up by the altar. I'm going to fix that."

"Ay José, what are you going to do? They'll kill us!"

"What does that matter? Jesus belongs up there, not animals. And death is a small thing. Heaven is what really matters."

He slipped out of the baptistery again and approached the bird sitting atop the tabernacle. Seeing him coming, the animal strutted about, but kept to its perch. As José stepped up level with the tabernacle, he spied a rope tying the rooster's foot to a brick. Reaching for the brick, he fiddled with the knot until it came undone. *I'll just let it go,* he thought, *and clean the tabernacle.*

He made as if to release the rope, then stopped. *And what's to stop it from coming back and making a mess again*?

Taking care to move slowly, José grabbed the animal and lifted it off the tabernacle top, bringing its body under his arm. Holding its body with his right hand, he wrapped his left hand around its head, pinning its beak closed. Then he gave one firm tug, causing its neck to break. The bird burst into a fit of flapping. Half a minute later, it hung limp. He tossed the body to the ground.

Turning around, he made quick work of the other two animals. Then he stripped off his shirt and used it to clear the muck and feathers from the altar and the tabernacle.

"That's better," he said, surveying the scene. "I wonder whose birds they were?"

"Imbecile! Do you know how much those birds were worth?"

Rafael Picazo tightened his grip around José's throat, holding the boy pinned to the rough brick wall. Lorenzo cowered in the corner.

José pulled against the vise-like hands, struggling desperately for breath, feet dangling. Without warning, Picazo let go, causing him to crash in a heap to the ground.

Still gasping, José carefully inched his way up the wall until he stood on his feet.

"Answer me!" bellowed the angry man, glaring down at him.

José opened his mouth and spoke. "*Padrino…*"

"Don't call me that! I'm not your *padrino* anymore."

José could see the veins bulging on Picazo's neck. He hesitated.

"I said 'Answer me!' " growled the man.

Clenching and unclenching his fists, José looked over at the altar of the church.

"The house of God is a place for prayer," he said, shaking his head, "not animals."

Picazo slammed his fist down on the marble baptismal font. "You little fiend! I gave you a chance to escape, and this is how you repay me? Your life is worth nothing to me now!" he shrieked.

José could see the soldier at Picazo's slide playing with the bolt on his rifle. His own knees started to tremble. Swallowing hard, he unclenched his fists. "Then go ahead, I'm ready," he said, almost whispering. "Shoot me if you like and send me to my God, so I can ask him to confound you."

The soldier at Picazo's side stepped forward, slamming his fist into José's jaw. "Cállate," the man snapped.

The blow sent José staggering. Blood flowed down his face. Leaning over, he coughed and tried to spit. Two of his teeth landed with the blood on the floor.

Sobbing came from where Lorenzo sat huddled.

Picazo turned on his heel, motioned to the soldier, and marched off.

32

Tía Magdalena

Later that evening, footsteps sounded again in the church.

"Someone's coming," said Lorenzo nervously.

José peered through the baptistery doorway.

"Someone in white… not a soldier… *Tía Magdalena* ?"

José's aunt strode into the baptistery unaccompanied.

"How did you get here?" he asked, giving her a hug.

"Let's just say I'm a neutral party," she said, peering into José's face. "What happened to your cheek boy? Is that a bruise I see? And your teeth…"

José lifted his hand up. "Picazo came… the soldier hit me."

"My dear boy," said the woman, giving him a hug, "we have to get you out of this place—both of you."

She drew a bag from her purse. "I brought you some food. There's rice and beans, a little chicken, and *agua de Jamaica*."

"You're the best, *Tía*," said José, accepting the gifts.

"And you are brave," she replied. "José, your father is on his way from Guadalajara to speak with Picazo."

The boy's face lit up.

"He wants to get you out of here—maybe he'll—"

"Visiting time's over," said a voice from the corridor.

Magdalena sighed. "You take care of yourself. If you have any messages, send them to *Tía Maria*. Goodbye." She hugged both boys and disappeared round a corner.

"My, my," said José, digging around in the bag of food. "*Tía Magdalena* always outdoes herself. She didn't mention the tamales and jalapeños she managed to sneak in here."

He poked around some more, then whistled. "Not to mention the churros. Come on Lorenzo, let's eat."

The other boy didn't move.

José took a bite from one of the churros.

"Heavenly," he murmured.

Lorenzo crossed his arms. "Your Papá is coming to rescue you," he said, "but my parents don't even know where I am."

José paused with the churro just inches from his lips.

"I'm sure that if they did know, they'd come for you too," he said, using his snack as a pointer. "Who knows, maybe my Papá can get us both out."

Lorenzo was motionless.

"Here, have some food," said José, holding out the cinnamon-and-sugar covered churro.

"I can't eat, I feel terrible," replied his friend.

José stopped and ran a hand through his buzz-cut black hair. Then he lowered himself to the ground beside Lorenzo.

"*Amigo,* all the pain will be gone in the blink of an eye, but heaven is forever."

His friend sat still.

"Come on. At least say grace with me."

"OK," answered Lorenzo.

"*Bendícenos, Señor, y bendice estos alimentos que por tu bondad vamos a tomar, por Cristo, nuestro Señor, Amén.*"

"Tastes good," murmured José, who had finished a second churro and started on the tamales. "Dinner's always better when you start with dessert."

Lorenzo peeked into Aunt Magdalena's bag of goodies.

Only the sound of munching came from José's direction.

"Alright," said Lorenzo, finally smiling, "you win. Let's try some of that chicken."

Both boys grabbed a drumstick.

"I wonder how those roosters would have tasted," mused Lorenzo between mouthfuls.

"Who knows," replied José, smiling to reveal his two missing teeth. "They felt kind of rubbery to me."

"Let go of him!" shouted José.

Morning had come, and with it four soldiers had stormed into the baptistery and roughly dragged the two boys out into the town square. Now an officer was slipping a noose around Lorenzo's neck.

"One more peep and you'll regret it," barked a soldier, jabbing a rifle barrel into José's back.

Lorenzo was crying now, even as the Lieutenant stood him on a little stool and tied the other end of the rope around the low-hanging branch of a cedar tree.

For a moment, the boy squirmed to free himself, but then the officer gave a kick to the stool, and his body shot down. He swayed back and forth a little, and went limp.

Burning-hot tears stole down José's cheeks in thick rivulets. He opened his mouth to scream, but choked on his own tongue. Every muscle in his body tensed up, waiting for his turn.

He watched as they lowered the small body of his friend down from the tree and loosened the rope from his neck. One of the soldiers pulled out a clasp knife and cut the cord that held Lorenzo's hands together. "Won't be doing much with those hands," he said, laughing.

Nearby stood a cart hitched to a donkey. Two of the soldiers grabbed Lorenzo's lifeless body and tossed him in like a potato sack.

The driver gave the donkey a whip and the cart rolled off in the direction of the cemetery.

José started. "Wait, what about me?" he asked nervously.

"I thought I told you to shut up," snapped the soldier. He reached a hand forward and struck José on the cheek, causing him to reel backwards.

"That'll teach you," jeered the man.

José watched the cart roll through the plaza until it turned the far corner and disappeared. Then the soldiers marched him back inside the church.

33

Ransom

"So nice to see you, Señor Sánchez," said Rafael Picazo from behind his massive oak desk.

Don Macario was still panting after jogging straight from the train station to Picazo's office. Brown dust clung to his white beard.

"Look, Señor Mayor," he said, once he had caught his breath a little, "This is a terrible mistake. José's no soldier. He doesn't belong in that prison."

"Ah, my dear Macario," replied Picazo. "I was inclined to think the same myself until I actually talked to the boy. I had assumed that the Cristeros tricked him into fighting. And of that I am still certain. But I also assumed that he didn't belong in prison. Last night, he destroyed some valuable property of mine. I know now that his insolence has gotten him exactly what he deserves."

"But Rafael, you're his *padrino,* for heaven's sake. Can't you just give the boy a chance? He's only fourteen."

"I gave him one chance," replied Picazo, "and he rejected it. Why should I give him another?"

"Because he's my son," replied Don Macario emphatically, "and I can't—I just can't lose him." He paused a moment, shaking his head. "Isn't there anything we can do?"

Rafael Picazo leaned back in his black leather chair and took a long pull on his cigar. Slowly releasing the smoke in one long plume, he stared Don Macario in the eyes.

"I won't even consider letting the boy go," he said, taking a deep breath, "until you pay the ransom."

"How much?"

"Oh, I don't know, something like five-thousand gold pesos," he said, letting the last words tumble off his lips like stones into a pond.

"*Jesús,*" mumbled Don Macario. "You know I don't have that kind of money."

"Well, if you value the little brat's life, then you'd better find someone who does."

In front of the baptismal font, José paced back and forth. Without Lorenzo, the night seemed to go on forever. *Why all the wait?*

"José, over here," said a voice at the window.

"Who's there?"

"It's me, Padre Ignacio."

José stood on the tips of his toes, barely managing to peer through the bars of the window.

"Boy am I glad it's you, Padre. What are you doing out in the open? If *los federales* see you—"

"Did you think I'd stay holed up in hiding when my favorite nephew was all alone in jail? Besides, I hope you've been taking good care of the church for me. They're keeping you prisoner here, but I'm not allowed near it."

"Ummm… let's just say that maybe you're better off not knowing what it's like in here," replied José.

"I figured as much. But tell me, we heard about poor little Lorenzo. How are you holding up?"

"Down a few teeth," began José, "but I'll be ok. I made up a song."

"You?"

"Yeah, a song about going to heaven," replied the boy. "It goes like this: 'to heaven, to heaven, to heaven I shall go.' "

"Oh José, not yet. You have your whole life ahead of you."

"I don't know. Watching Lorenzo really made me wonder. I felt like I was ready to go along with him. I don't know why they took him and not me."

"You are one brave nephew," said the priest. "I wish I had half the guts you do."

"Come on Padre, I'm not a hero," said José, blushing. "What have you been up to?"

"Oh, mostly saying Mass in people's homes and trying to keep up their hopes," said the priest with a sigh.

José's eyes brightened. "If you can say Mass, do you think I could receive communion?" he asked.

"I don't know. This window's too high for me to bring it to you." The priest thought for a minute. "Maybe we could smuggle it in with your food or something."

"Yeah," said José excitedly. "Tía Magdalena brings me food sometimes."

"OK, next time she comes—" the priest broke off. "Someone's coming. God bless you, son."

In the corner office high above the town square, two men sat talking.

"But Rafael, just think about the money."

"*No me importa*. I'll get rid of the boy whether or not Sánchez coughs up the ransom. You do your job, and you'll receive your pay."

"Whatever you say," replied the man, tinkering with the pistol in his hands.

"My soldiers will bring the boy to the old rendezvous this evening," said Picazo, giving a pull on his cigar. "After the bell rings for curfew, he's all yours. I don't care how you do it, or what you use. All I ask is that come sunrise, there's another body in the graveyard."

Later that evening four soldiers marched into the church, tied José by the hands, and pushed him outside. As soon as his feet touched the dust of the town square, his eyes shot to the cedar tree where Lorenzo had been hanged. But no noose hung from its branches.

They walked him past the tree, and then down the south side of the square, turning left at the corner. After a few more steps, they came to a halt at the door of *El Meson*, an old inn. The blinds of the building were drawn and on the façade wooden lathing showed through missing chinks of plaster.

The soldier in front shoved the door open.

"In here with the boy," he said.

The light from his lantern cast wavelike shadows down the walls within. In the middle of the room sat a long wooden table. Covered in cobwebs, a ramshackle chandelier dangled from the ceiling. Small piles of clutter were spread about the floor, much the same as at the church.

"What are you going to do with me?" asked José.

"You sit down here," said the soldier, motioning to a place beside the wall, "and keep quiet."

José shuffled over, hands still tied together, and carefully slid down the wall until he sat cross-legged on the damp floor.

Back and forth, back and forth the soldiers walked, never speaking a word.

After what felt like a small eternity, there came a knock. One of the soldiers hurried over and swung the door inward.

"On your feet, prisoner," snapped a soldier.

José looked up, just in time to see his *padrino* enter the room.

"Everything in order men?" asked Picazo, tossing the stub of a cigar to the ground and grinding it under his heel.

"Yes sir, Señor Mayor," said the man who had been carrying the lantern.

"Bueno."

He walked up to the table and stopped just opposite José. After fumbling around in his pocket, he extracted a small piece of parchment.

"Let me see," he said, twisting one side of his moustache. His eyes scanned the paper.

Without raising them, he continued, "Aha, just as I thought:

> The committee has issued a sentence as regards one José Sánchez del Río, member of the insurrectionary force in open war with our esteemed government. For having been found guilty of high treason, the aforementioned rebel is to be put to death, without delay, to serve as an example to any who may feel inclined to join in so odious and unpatriotic an undertaking.

He slowly folded the paper and slipped it back into his pocket.

"They'll come for the boy at half-past eight," said Picazo to the soldiers. "I want you to accompany them—make sure there are no mistakes."

José stared intently at Picazo's face. It betrayed no emotion—not even a twitch.

After a weighty silence, the Mayor turned to leave.

Just before he reached the door, José blurted out, "Can I send for a last meal?"

Picazo stopped. For a moment he was silent, as if hovering between two worlds. Then the moment passed.

"You," he said, motioning to the soldier nearest the door, "bring the prisoner pen and paper."

"And you," he continued, addressing another soldier. "Tell Zamorano that I want it done quietly—no bullets."

With that, he stepped through the doorway and out into the darkening night.

34
Last Communion

Señora

María Sanchez de Olmedo

My Very Dear Aunt,

I've been sentenced to death. At 8:30 the moment I have waited so long for will arrive. Thank you so much for all the favors that you and Tía Magdalena did for me. I don't feel like I can write my mother. Can you please write her and María for me? The Lieutenant says Aunt Magdalena can come once more, can you please tell her? I think she'll come.

Say goodbye to everyone for me, and just like always and last of all, I give you all my love - you know how much I love you and want to see you.

Christ lives, Christ reigns, Christ rules. Viva Cristo Rey y Santa María de Guadalupe.

José Sanchez del Río who died in defense of his faith.

Don't forget to come.

Farewell.

Trembling, José set down the pen. His heart beat relentlessly against his chest as he slid the letter into the envelope.

Seeing that he had finished, the soldier on duty grabbed the letter with a grunt. After glancing at the name, he slipped from the room.

The other three soldiers stayed in their places.

Only ten minutes after he had sealed the letter, José heard voices outside.

"Can I see the boy? He's my nephew."

"Sorry Señora, we've got orders," said the soldier. "I'll just have to take that bundle for you."

"Men," fumed the woman. She pushed the soldier aside and stuck her head through the doorway.

"I'm sorry Señora, you're not allowed to—"

"Not allowed to do what?" she snapped. "And you, Pedro Torres," she continued, facing inside, "is this what I get for all the times I bandaged your scraped knees, and carried you back to your mother? I would have thought better of you."

"Pedro, don't let her," said the soldier at the door.

"But—" the other replied, shrugging his shoulders.

The man at the door threw his hands up in the air.

"Alright Señora Magdalena, you can come in, but make it short."

"That's better," she said adamantly, and stepped inside.

José, who had been watching the scene unfold in silence, rose to his feet.

"You got my message?" he asked apprehensively.

She made as if to reply, then swung around to see three pairs of eyes and ears fixed in their direction.

"What about a little privacy?" she asked indignantly.

"Señora, we have to report to the Mayor."

"What kind of cruel men are you?" she demanded. "This is my nephew. Go on; step outside for a moment so my nephew and I can have a little heart-to-heart talk."

Grumbling to each other, the soldiers made their way out the door.

"Finally," she said, turning to José. "My dear boy…" she started, then gave a sigh and stretched her arms out, enveloping him in one big hug.

"Thanks for coming, Tía Magdalena," was all he could say.

"Oh José," she said, looking him in the eyes. "Are you sure you want to go through with this?"

"I—I think so," he replied. "I've already been sentenced."

She let out a sigh. "I know, I know, my boy. But you do know that you're always free." She dropped her voice to a whisper, "I talked to the man who owns this building. He says there's a way out the back." She pointed to the door on their left.

José nodded.

"Was there anything else?" she asked.

"Did you bring—"

The look of concern passed from Aunt Magdalena's face. She smiled, and nodded, taking a small golden container from the bundle she was carrying.

"The body of Christ," she said, holding up the little white host.

A look of deep release spread across José's face and lit up his features. "Amen."

35

Empty Promise

The gold coins spilled from the sack and across the table onto the floor. Each piece glittered profusely in the candlelight.

"Five thousand. You can count it out: I'm sure it's there. Had to sell my house—and everything else."

"Impressive, Macario," said Rafael Picazo. "I admit I didn't think you quite up to the task."

Don Macario faked a smile. His fingers shone white as they clung tightly to the sack from which he had poured the coins. Dark bags hung from his eyes, and his shoes were caked with dust. His beard had grown scraggly and grey.

"It's all yours," he said. "Now—now give me my boy."

Picazo got to his feet and grabbed a handful of coins. He shook them back and forth in his palm, listening to the merry ring.

"You must understand me, Don Macario, when I say that these things take time," he stated somberly. "I'll need to file for a stay of execution, then if that's granted—"

"*If*?" exclaimed Don Macario. "You never told us there had been a sentence. For heaven's sake Rafael," here he dropped his voice, "this is my son. Just let him go."

"Ah, Don Macario," said Picazo. "If only you would have chosen the right side in the first place, maybe now your son wouldn't be in such a precarious position."

"Rafael, listen to me," Don Macario pleaded, drawing closer to the Mayor. "Maybe you're right. Maybe I did make a mistake." He paused, laying a hand on his chest. "I can't change that now. But I can guarantee you that if you give me back my son, he won't cause you any more trouble."

Rafael Picazo smiled. Setting the coins down, he opened the top drawer of his desk and slowly pulled out two cigars. After lighting them both, he handed one to Don Macario, who accepted it with knit brow.

"Orderly," he called.

"A sus órdenes," answered a soldier who had been stationed down the hallway.

"Please show Señor Sánchez downstairs."

The man nodded.

Don Macario hesitated, and then followed him into the hall, cigar still smoking in his hand.

José watched his aunt step through the front door and into the night. From outside came voices—probably Aunt Magdalena giving another lecture to the soldiers.

Her last words echoed in his head. Turning to his left he faced the doorway she had talked of. Now was his chance. He could escape and return to fight with the Cristeros.

He slipped over to the door. With a little pressure, the handle turned smoothly. Glancing over his shoulder he took one last look. Aunt Magdalena's voice still drifted through the air, but no one had entered the room yet.

His heart was pounding furiously against his ribcage. "Come on, come on," he whispered as he pushed on the door, hoping the hinges wouldn't squeak.

The door swung inward and a second later he had stepped into a dark chamber. At the far end, he could see two more doors outlined against the wall. "The one on the right," Aunt Magdalena had drilled into his head.

José stepped forward. Simultaneously the door behind him swung shut and pitched the room into total darkness.

He kept his eyes turned toward where he had seen the door before and kept walking. Sure enough, after maybe ten steps, he could feel its outline.

Just a light push and he had stepped into a small courtyard. Still throbbing like a freight train, his heart now felt like it was lodged in his throat.

Far above, a half-moon shone brightly in the dark night sky, casting down an eerie light, enough for José to see a few small trees and potted plants scattered about the courtyard.

As he took another step forward, images suddenly came roaring through his mind. *A shot, loud as dynamite, rent the summer air. The figure in black tumbled to the ground. No! Shouts a boy. He wants to scream but the noise is choked in his throat by the hot dust and by his own tears…*

"No."

Suddenly his legs buckled. He felt an urgent need to use the bathroom. The nearest tree looked welcoming.

At the same instant, someone began to shout from behind the door. The soldiers were back.

"This way," bawled a voice from the other side. Moments later, with a crash the door came flying open. A lantern cast its beams out into the night.

"There he is," shouted the voice. "You boy, what do you think you're doing?" barked the man as he rushed over.

José turned to face the soldier. "Using the bathroom," he said.

36

Zero Hour

"What do you have to say for yourself?"

"Yeah, come on, you're just a little boy."

"You don't have to die."

"All you have to say is 'Long live President Calles', and we'll let you go."

Once the soldiers had brought José back to the room, they placed him in the corner under guard. An hour later, the curfew bell rang, and a gang of men arrived at the door. Out of their belts peeked revolvers, and on their faces lurked twisted sneers. After a little nodding and pointing, the soldiers let them in.

They had quickly drawn up in a semicircle around José.

"So what do you say, little boy?" said a man with a scraggly beard. "You'd better choose carefully, 'cause my switchblade don't like the looks of you," he taunted, dangling the knife in José's face.

"Yeah, speak up," said another, whose breath stunk of Tequila. "I got Aztec blood in me and I ain't afraid to use it."

"Come on son," continued a third, who was taller and more muscular than the rest. " 'Long live President Calles'—that's all you have to say."

I don't even have to escape, he thought. *Just four words and I'm free.*

Then his own advice to Lorenzo came echoing back in his ears, "The pain will be gone in the blink of an eye, but heaven is forever."

"Viva Cristo Rey," said José.

WHACK!

No sooner had he closed his lips than the biggest of the thugs backhanded him across the face.

"You sure about that?" the man demanded.

The blow jammed José's molars deep into his cheek. As he turned to face the mob again, a drop of blood trickled down his chin. He slowly wiped it away, and stared at the streak of blood on his hand in silence.

Then he nodded.

Rough hands grabbed at him from every direction.

"Wait. Put him on the table," said the big man.

"Yeah, time to have some fun," said the one with the switchblade.

"Lay him flat," said a voice. "It's easier to get at the feet that way."

The men lifted José from the ground and tossed him onto the table face down. His skull struck the top with a crack.

"Pispírria, you hold him down from that side," said the big man, pointing. "Chiscuasa, over here."

"Never been happier to help, Aguada," said the man, stepping to his place and sinking his fingers into José's arm.

"Time for some knife work," said the man with the scraggly beard. He stepped forward and grabbed José by the foot.

"Malpolá, wait," said Aguada. "Our little friend can't see what's going on. Turn him over."

The men tossed José onto his back.

"That's better," said Malpolá, fingering his knife. "Alright boy," he continued, leaning down into José's face, "we're going to play a little game. You're on trial, and my knife is the judge. Say what the judge likes to hear, and you go home, safe and sound. Say what the judge doesn't like to hear," he paused, looking around, "and he might just peel your feet like a ripe banana."

José frowned.

"Alright, what do you say to the judge little boy?"

José swallowed hard, his eyes intent on the razor-sharp knife. "The same thing I said before," he answered, thinking of his friend hanging from the tree. *"Viva Cristo Rey."*

"Should have listened," said Malpolá shaking his head. Grabbing José's right foot, he slashed at the bottom with his knife.

Pain shot up the leg. He wriggled and tried to move, but the men at both sides held him down, snickering all the while.

"What's the problem," sneered Pispírria, "change your mind all of a sudden?"

With teeth clenched, José glared at the man.

"I don't like that look," said Malpolá. He grabbed José's other foot and this time slowly dragged his knife down the sole, peeling the top layer of skin away.

"What do you say now?" he demanded as he pulled his blade away.

José writhed back and forth with all his might, but the men gripped him like a vise. Blood dripped down his feet and gathered in pools on the table. Both feet felt like they were on fire.

"Aw, come on Malpolá," barked Aguada, "look at the mess you're making. Let the prisoner stand on his own two feet."

"Wait," said one of the men who had been watching from the side. "Better disinfect the wounds." His hand grasped a small burlap sack. Undoing a string, he let fall a stream of small white rocks and dust. Then he used his boot to spread it around the floor at the base of the table.

"Just what the doctor ordered—rock salt," said Malpolá. "Change your mind yet?" he asked, turning to José.

By now the men had lifted José to a sitting position on the edge of the table. He could see the white carpet strewn before him. His cheeks shone wet with tears and blood.

"No," he stammered, shaking his head. *"Viva Cristo Rey."*

The men hoisted José off the table and jammed his feet down into the salt. He let out a gasp of pain and tried to draw up his legs. Their brawny arms only pushed him down harder.

"Alright gentlemen," said Aguada, looking around. "Time to march this sorry little excuse for a soldier—that is, unless he has something to say."

José was still wriggling and wincing in pain.

"What's that, have you had enough?" asked Aguada.

The boy nodded.

In the living room of the Sánchez del Río house in Guadalajara, Doña Mariquita sat by her youngest daughter.

"Mamá, do you think Papá will bring José back?" asked the little girl.

"Oh Celia," replied Doña Mariquita, fiddling with her needlework, "I certainly hope so. Papá will do anything it takes."

"But what if José doesn't want to come?"

"What do you mean, sweetie?"

"You remember what José said when he told us he was leaving, right?"

"He said a lot of things."

"Yes, but I remember one thing especially," she replied. "Before José went off to join the Cristeros, he said, 'Winning heaven has never been so easy.' "

Mariquita set her stitching on the coffee table and sat down beside the little girl.

"Celia dear, how did you hear that?"

The little girl cocked her head to the side.

"Because we were all on the stairs, listening, when he told you and Papá."

"I should have known," groaned Doña Mariquita.

"It'll be ok Mamá," said Celia. "Just a day or two, and I'll have a brother in heaven."

Doña Mariquita took Celia in her arms.

"Celia dear, how can you say such a thing? Papá will bring José back safe and sound."

"Oh Mamá, you don't understand, do you? God gave you three daughters and four sons."

"What does that have to do with it, *tesoro*?" asked Doña Mariquita, looking deep into Celia's eyes.

"He gave you three daughters and three sons for this earth," answered the little girl, grasping her mother's neck, "and one for heaven."

37

Calvary Road

"Let's go boy, on your feet. I thought you said you'd had enough!"

José lay sprawled in the dust of the street before the doorway of *El Meson*. When he had again refused to comply with Aguada's demands, the group had shoved him out the entrance, where he lost his balance. With his hands still tied behind his back, there was nothing to stop his fall but the dirt. Luckily he had landed rolling, and now lay on his side.

"*Que pasa,* Cristero boy can't even keep his balance?" snickered Chiscuasa.

The men and the soldiers stood in a crescent around the fallen boy.

With hands still tied behind his back, José twisted his torso and managed to rise to a sitting position. But no

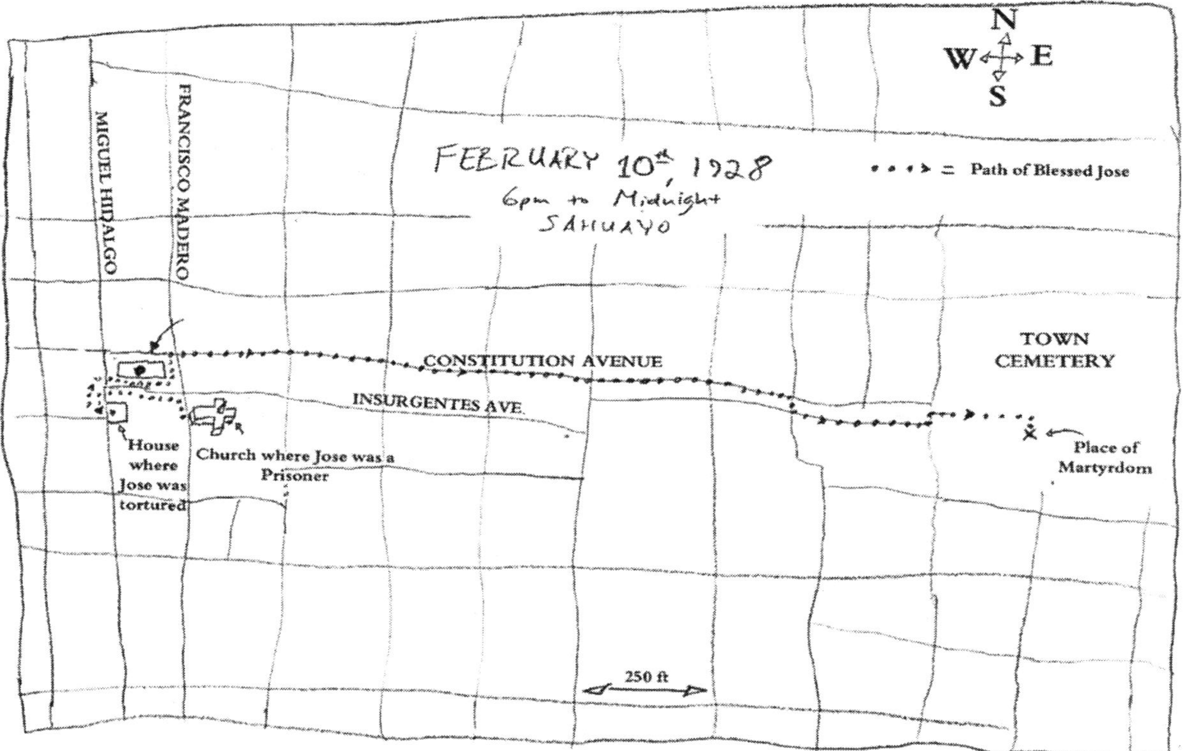
N
W
E
S
FEBRUARY 10th, 1928
6pm to Midnight
SAHUAYO
• • • > = Path of Blessed Jose
MIGUEL HIDALGO
FRANCISCO MADERO
CONSTITUTION AVENUE
INSURGENTES AVE.
TOWN CEMETERY
House where Jose was tortured
Church where Jose was a Prisoner
Place of Martyrdom
250 ft

sooner had he started pushing with his feet to stand up than the sickening pain made him stop. This caused an uproar of laughter.

"Shut your traps boys, Picazo wants us to keep this quiet," said Aguada menacingly. The laughter died down.

By now José was using his head to lift himself up. He pressed it into the dust and dirt, and managed to rise to his knees. It felt better resting on them than his feet.

He lifted his right leg and ever so slowly set his foot upon the ground. The pain caused by the mix of dirt and salt in the open wound made him lurch sideways and almost fall again.

"Alright, march," said Aguada.

José took one step forward. The terrible burning sensation shooting up from his feet made him stumble again. He hopped from foot to foot, but instead of lessening, the pain only grew worse. He wanted to cry out.

"What kind of soldier are you?" asked Pispírria mockingly. "I knew the Cristeros were just a bunch of women."

"Viva Cristo Rey."

"Look boy," said Aguada, "I told you not to say that."

"I say we make him pay for every word he says," declared Malpolá, weapon still in hand.

He took a slash at José's shirt. The sharp blade slid across the boy's side. Blood came soaking through. Doubled over by the pain, José barely managed to catch his balance.

Malpolá made as if to slash again, but Aguada grabbed his hand.

"*Basta,*" he said. "Wait till the cemetery."

Rafael Picazo stood at the window of his third floor office overlooking the town square.

He glanced at his watch. 11:15. They were behind schedule.

"How hard is it to get rid of one little boy?" he wondered aloud.

He scanned the square again. The lampposts cast pools of yellow light on the streets beneath. Nothing moved.

He was proud of those lampposts—they were his first project as mayor, back before the war. Once the Cristeros were all dead and gone, he had plans for beautifying and modernizing Sahuayo even more.

Something moved in the far corner of the square. Picazo sidled up to the window and gazed out.

"*Tonto,*" he said.

He could see the ring of soldiers around José. Aguada lead, Malpolá with his knife took the rear, and soldiers marched on either side with rifles at their hips.

Through the open window came the noise of shouting.

"*Idiotas* better keep quiet or the whole town will be out to see."

The clamor grew louder as the procession wound its way across the south side of the square and then headed north.

Picazo listened from his window. It wasn't the soldiers who were making the noise.

"Viva Cristo Rey."

The blood drained from his face. *"No puede ser."* He slammed his fist down on the desk. "Of all the God-forsaken places I could be, they had to put me here!"

He rushed out of his office and headed for the stairs. As he pulled open the front door of the building, he saw the group turning the corner to head east out of the square and down Constitution Avenue.

"Aguada!" he shouted, hurrying down the front steps.

The soldiers stopped, as did the men in front and back.

"I thought I told you to keep it quiet," Picazo remonstrated.

"We're not making the noise, your godson is," the man answered.

Picazo cursed and then pushed his way past the soldiers.

José turned to face him.

"Look boy, I've already been too nice with you. I'm giving you one last chance. Say '*Qué muere Cristo rey*', or you'll wish you had later."

José opened his mouth as if to speak, but no words came.

"*Qué pasa*?" demanded Picazo, scorn dripping from his voice.

"Ni idea," answered Aguada. "Maybe you finally convinced him."

José's eyes were fixed on a spot just to the left of Picazo's shoulder.

"Answer me boy—now!"

"Padre Ignacio?"

"Trino, what are you doing here?"

"When I heard about José's capture, I had to come."

"I was just going to see how the boy's doing myself," said the priest. "This is no hour for you to be out in the streets though."

"You too, Padre. But we'll be safer together."

"Alright then—follow me."

Padre Ignacio rounded the corner of Tepeyac street with Trino at his heels. So it was that José saw his uncle and his friend appear out of nowhere.

"Wait," whispered Padre Ignacio, "get down."

Trino dove and rolled, spreading a cloud of dust across his wake. Luckily for him, Mayor Picazo had installed lamps only in the town square. The darkness of the side street was their friend right now.

"Good thinking," whispered Trino. "Who are all those men?"

"Los malos," said Padre Ignacio. "the *Acordada* – Picazo's henchmen ."

Shouts carried down the street.

"Sounds like Picazo," said Trino.

"Hush, I'm trying to hear."

They both cupped their hands around their ears.

"So what's your answer, boy?" snarled an indignant voice.

"The same one I gave before: *Viva Cristo Rey y Santa María de Guadalupe*!"

"Give me that rifle," barked Picazo to one of the soldiers.

CRACK!

Padre Ignacio and Trino winced as he brought the rifle crashing into the side of José's jaw.

"That'll keep you quiet," he barked.

Trino was livid.

"That's it, I'm going in there," he said, getting to his feet.

Padre Ignacio grabbed him by the shoulder. "No you're not," he said. "They'll kill you too."

Trino dropped back down on one knee.

"Look," said Padre Ignacio, pointing. "There goes Picazo back to his den. They've started moving again."

"Let's follow them," Trino suggested.

"OK," answered the priest, starting off.

They hung close to the wall, watching as the group of soldiers left the square and headed down Constitution Street. By the time Trino and the padre reached the place where Picazo had hit José, the ruffians were already a block away.

"Look," said Trino, stooping down and placing a hand on the ground. "José's footprints—they're red."

Padre Ignacio gasped.

"Murderers."

38

Trial by Water

"What's wrong, *niño*?"

A long trail of red ran down José's front from mouth to shirt. He hobbled along between the soldiers, shifting from foot to foot, trying to keep his balance. The cemetery wall was drawing closer with every step.

"Come on kid, get a move on it," growled Malpolá. He shoved José from behind.

"Sounds like he's ready to give up," said the man, tossing his knife from one hand to the other. "Let's help him."

Pivoting backwards, Malpolá whirled around, bringing his knife in a diagonal slash across José's back. The boy couldn't stifle his scream.

"Give up now?" snickered Malpolá.

José limped along, following the men in front.

Malpolá smirked and prepared to make another go.

Just then, Aguada raised a hand, motioning everyone to stop. Malpolá checked his knife.

"What do you think, would some water help convince him?" asked Aguada. He pointed to the cemetery wall looming ahead. "How about the old well?"

"We'll need rope," observed Chiscuasa.

"*He aquí*," chimed in Zamorano, pulling a dirty ball of twine from his pocket.

"Tie him by his feet," said Pispírria.

They halted by the cemetery wall.

"Hey, Malpolá, help me move the lid," said Chiscuasa.

With a little wrenching and grinding the circular stone slid away, revealing a sizeable hole in the ground.

"Hold still boy," said Zamorano, stooping down and slipping the rope around José's feet.

"Zamorano, what if your twine snaps on us?" asked Aguada.

"I doubled it up," answered the man, as he gave a finishing touch to his knot. "Besides, the kid knows how to swim."

Aguada nodded. "Alright boy," he said, "we're going to give you some time to think. Have a drink while you're at it."

Chiscuasa and Pispírria dropped José to the ground, and dragged him to the side of the hole. Zamorano still held onto the end of the twine. He nodded. With a shove they pushed José over the edge.

Water splashed up the sides of the well and onto the ground.

"Water's high tonight," said Zamorano, bracing his legs.

"Stupid boy," said Chiscuasa, "escape is so easy."

"Yeah, if his head weren't as hard as those gravestones," added Malpolá with a laugh.

More water splashed over the sides of the well.

"Maybe the dip has knocked some sense into him," said Pispírria.

"That enough, Aguada?" asked Zamorano, still holding onto the twine.

"Un poco más."

"Wouldn't want to cut his swim short," said Malpolá.

"What do we do if the boy gives in?" asked Chiscuasa.

"Send him back to Picazo," answered Aguada, "that is, if he's still alive."

The men all snickered.

"It's been about a minute, right?" asked Aguada.

"I don't feel movement anymore," declared Zamorano, rope in hand.

"Ya basta."

Zamorano yanked. "Give me some help, the kid's heavy," he said.

Chiscuasa and Pispírria reached into the hole as Zamorano heaved. Water gushed out, as first José's legs, and then the rest of his body appeared.

"What's wrong niño, didn't like your swim?" Malpolá jeered.

"Shut up," snapped Chiscuasa, bending over the motionless body. "He's unconscious."

He rolled José onto his back. The boy's face shone pale blue.

One of the soldiers staggered over. "Push on his chest," he said.

Chiscuasa placed both his hands across José's chest and shoved.

Nothing happened.

"Again," said the soldier.

Still nothing.

"Here, let me try."

The soldier placed his hands atop the boy and began pushing rhythmically.

"Picazo will have our necks if he dies here," said Aguada.

The soldier looked up. "I need somebody to breath into his mouth," he said.

With a curse, Chiscuasa bent down and placed his lips on the boy's. He breathed out.

"OK, keep it up," directed the soldier, who was still pushing on the boy's chest.

Pispírria tossed his knife into the ground and sighed. "Didn't think he'd go that quick."

Suddenly, José's chest shuddered. The two men stopped their work.

"What happened?" demanded Aguada.

"Wait," replied the soldier, lifting the boy to a sitting position.

José choked, then vomited down his shirt. Opening his eyes, he coughed and started heaving in lungfuls of air.

"Set him on his feet," ordered Aguada.

Chiscuasa and the soldier lifted José's body up. For a moment he wobbled between the two men. Then he caught his balance.

Aguada held his lantern up to José's swollen, half-blue face. "What do you have to say for yourself now?"

"Padre Ignacio, what are you doing here alone?"

"I'm not alone, Señora Magdalena" said the priest, ducking down behind the cemetery wall.

The sound of footsteps revealed Trino, who appeared out of the darkness and sat down beside the priest.

"What's happening?" asked Trino. "I can't see."

"They just tried to drown José in the cemetery well," replied the woman.

"No!" exclaimed Trino.

"He's back on his feet now," she said.

The boy got to his knees and peered over the low rock wall. The noise of men shouting came drifting over the wind.

"What's that boy? Couldn't hear you—"

One of the men shoved José from behind.

"Speak a little louder!"

They could hear José's cough—the same pitch as always—just weaker now.

"*Viva—*" came his shaky voice, "*—Viva Cristo Rey.*"

They heard a loud thump and saw José fall forward.

Padre Ignacio covered his face with his hands.

Tears poured down Trino's cheeks.

"He doesn't have much longer," whispered Tía Magdalena.

39

Winning Heaven

"Where's that gravedigger?" demanded Aguada.

"Over here sir," said a voice from the middle of the graveyard.

The men marched off, pushing José from behind.

As they arrived at where the old man stood, Aguada threw up his hands in impatience.

"Where's the grave?"

"Orders of Señor Picazo sir," replied the man. "The prisoner is to dig his own grave. I'm only allowed to fill it in."

Aguada laughed. "The Mayor sure has imagination."

"Here's a shovel," said the gravedigger, holding out a small spade.

"You heard the man, boy. Get to work," Aguada demanded.

Wet and shivering, José hobbled forward, hands tied behind his back.

"You might want to free the prisoner's hands," observed the gravedigger.

"Mind your own business," snapped Aguada. He turned and signaled to Malpolá.

The man lumbered over and grabbed José by the wrists. A quick slice, and the rope fell to the ground.

José slowly brought his arms forward until they hung like weights at his side.

"OK boy," shouted Malpolá, giving José a kick from behind, "start digging!"

José reeled forward. The gravedigger reached out to stop him from falling and grabbed him with both arms. Then he set the boy back on his feet. Trembling himself, he took first one, then the other of José's hands and wrapped them around the handle of the shovel. Then he pointed to an "x" marked on the ground.

José feebly scraped at the dirt.

"Looks like he could use some encouragement," said Malpolá, knife at the ready.

Aguada held up a hand.

At first José only scratched ineffectively at the soil. Then ever so slowly, he managed to grip the shovel tighter. Blood began to flow back into his fingers. Each scoop removed a little pile of dirt.

The cloud was clearing from his mind now. *I'm digging my grave. My own grave,* he thought. *Heaven. Almost there. Almost.* He paused, suddenly feeling nauseated, and placed a hand on his stomach.

"Snap out of it boy," shouted Aguada.

He gripped the shovel again and resumed the digging. *José,* said a little voice in his head, *you don't have to do this. You've already suffered enough. Just give in, walk away. You can still be a Cristero.*

José peered around. The men were all still there, laughing and joking. Where did the voice come from?

Just drop the shovel and walk away, it said. *It's so easy.*

José shook his head, trying to think clearly. *Why is this happening?* he asked himself. He pulled another shovelful of dirt from the ground. *I've got to stop the voice.*

With a mighty thrust, he sunk the shovel deep into the ground. Leaning against the handle with all his weight, he drew out the dirt.

Then he swallowed and opened his lips. "I need to pray," he whispered.

"Viva Cristo Rey."

"What's that boy?" asked Malpolá.

"Viva Cristo Rey," answered José.

"Shut up and get digging," snapped Aguada.

"Viva Cristo Rey," José stated emphatically.

The men drew closer round the boy, who continued his digging.

"Viva Cristo Rey," he said, louder this time.

"Basta," said Malpolá.

He nodded to Pispírria. They both pulled out their knives, as did Chiscuasa and Zamorano.

"Viva Cristo Rey!" said José, almost chanting now.

Aguada nodded.

"Have a taste of this," sneered Malpolá, bringing his knife down hard on the boy's shoulder.

José gasped. The shovel fell from his arms and clattered to the ground. He staggered, then turning around, gazed at the men with their weapons. "No matter what you do to me," he said, grasping his shoulder, "every time I move it means '*Viva Cristo Rey.*' "

The men stepped forward, closing the knot tight around the boy. Without waiting, they let their weapons rain down on his small body.

A knife tore open a long gash down his right arm, another pierced his leg.

"How does that feel?" asked Pispírria as he pulled his blade, dripping with blood, away.

"*Viva Cristo Rey,*" said José, between labored gasps.

"I've had enough of this," stated Malpolá. He slashed again, this time slicing through José's shirt and cutting a gash in his chest.

"Give up yet?" the infuriated man demanded.

The blow had knocked José down on his back. He scrambled to his knees and stared at the blood dripping down his arms and over his hands. Leaning over he dragged his bloody finger in the dust, first sideways, then up and down. A bloody cross. Then, carefully, painfully he repeated his cry, "*Viva Cristo Rey, y Santa María de Guadalupe*"

Aguada walked up behind the kneeling boy. In his palm sat a small wooden-handled pistol.

"*Niño,* what do you want me to tell your father?" he asked, slowly raising his weapon.

Joining his hands together, as if in prayer, José raised his head.

"*Qué nos veremos en el cielo* - That we'll see each other in heaven."

Then, taking a deep breath, he added, "*Viva Cristo Rey, y Santa María de Guadalupe*!"

Aguada stiffened. "*Basta!*" he barked, placing the barrel of his revolver just behind the right ear of the kneeling boy. His finger trembled for a moment, then squeezed.

It was half an hour to midnight, February 10th, 1928.

Epilogue

40

Ten Minutes Later

As the ruffians walked back laughing to report to Picazo, they were surprised to see people in the streets. There were people everywhere: people weeping, people kneeling, people gathering small handfuls of the damp red earth.

From every direction, their whispers echoed one word: "Martyr."

41

Two Days Earlier

"Here you go, old man, this one's freshly hanged," said the soldier, dropping the motionless little body at the entrance to the cemetery.

Luis Gómez looked at the soldier, then back at the little boy. He had dug more tombs in the past month than the previous fifteen years. But what were soldiers doing with the body of a boy?

"Where do you want the grave?" asked the soldier. "The boss told me to help you dig, if you need it."

The gravedigger laid a hand on the boy's neck. He could have used some help, but—what was that? He thought he could feel a slight pulse.

"Oh, *no te preocupes*. They need you in town. "I'll take care of him," he said, scratching his head.

The soldier smiled. “Thanks, gravedigger man. I owe you one.”

He jumped into the cart and gave the donkey a lash. The animal trotted off.

For a moment, Luis made as if to dig the grave. Once the soldier had disappeared from sight, he hurried back and bent over the body. Yes, there was a pulse, though weak.

“Stupid soldiers can’t even do a hanging right,” he murmured under his breath.

Unscrewing the lid of his canteen, he took the boy’s head in one hand, and with the other poured some water over Lorenzo’s face.

The head shook a little, and then the lips parted in a yawn. Moments later, the eyelids fluttered and opened. The gravedigger gave a chuckle.

“Here son, take a drink of this,” he said, holding out the canteen.

“Dónde… where am I?” asked the boy, rubbing his face.

“You should be in that hole,” answered the gravedigger, pointing.

A puzzled expression crossed Lorenzo’s face. “Where’s José?” he asked.

“You mean the Sánchez boy?”

“Yeah, him. We’re prisoners together in the church.”

The gravedigger shrugged. “What’s your name boy?” he inquired.

“Lorenzo.”

“Hmmm. I reckon we should give you a new name now.”

“Why’s that?”

"Because you, my friend, are one lucky boy. By all rights you should be lying under six feet of moist dirt right now. It's like you've been raised to life. We'll call you Lazarus."

"What next?" asked the boy, once he had gobbled down half the gravedigger's dinner.

"*Váyate,*" replied the old man. "Get as far away from Sahuayo as you can. If you head due south you'll make Jiquilpan or even Los Remedios tonight. I'll dig you a nice grave and bury a stick at the bottom. Those incompetent federal dogs will never know the difference."

42

Three Years Later

"Enrique, how much longer till Sahuayo?"

"Heck, Rafael, I don't know. I just want to get off this silly train."

"Me too."

"I'd trade México City for Sahuayo any day."

"So would I, but still, nothing beats being Mayor of Sahuayo. It's like I'm king."

"Ha, ha, and what a kingdom you have. Dusty streets, buildings falling apart, people who would shoot you dead on sight…"

"Oh please," snapped Rafael Picazo. "When you've got as much power as I do, you might start enjoying life. Until then, just let me do my job."

The train rumbled on. The two men sat in silence, staring out the window. Unnoticed to both, a third figure slipped into the compartment.

"Rafael Picazo?" asked the man.

Both men turned and stared at the newcomer. A look of surprise stole across Picazo's face.

"Manuel Gallardo—funny running into you here," he said uneasily.

"Then you must be the only one laughing, as usual," said the man, drawing a revolver from his belt.

Picazo scooted back against the wall of the compartment, cautiously raising his hands in the air.

"Whoa, wait a minute Manuel, we can talk about this," he protested.

"Talk?" asked the man. "I think we've talked enough. You can't seem to keep your nose out of my business, and I'm going to make sure you don't have another chance."

BANG! He fired six cartridges point blank into Picazo's chest. Then wheeling around, he opened the door and dashed down the corridor.

The shots came so quickly that neither man had a chance to shout for help. Now Enrique knelt at the side of his dying friend.

Rafael Picazo's body was shaking convulsively.

"Rafael, Rafael, stay with me," shouted Enrique.

Other passengers had heard the shots, and they started to gather now outside the open compartment's door.

"I, I, I want—" mumbled Picazo.

"Yes, yes, what is it?" asked Enrique, holding his friend's hand.

"I want a priest. Get me a priest," gasped the dying man.

"For God's sake Rafael, how am I supposed to find a priest here?"

"I am a priest," said a voice from behind them. Enrique turned and saw a man dressed like a peasant stepping from the crowd.

"I'm Padre Pablo Silva."

"Padre," whispered Rafael Picazo softly, "would you please hear my confession?"

43

Seventy-Seven Years Later

The sky shone blood-red in the rays of the setting sun. Not a seat was left in the soccer stadium today, November 20th, 2005. But no soccer players could be seen driving any balls down the grassy field. The crowd of 70,000 was cheering, but not for any athlete.

It was the beatification ceremony of thirteen martyrs, among them a fourteen-year-old boy from Sahuayo. He was being declared "blessed"—the last step before becoming a saint—along with the man at whose tomb he had prayed for the grace of martyrdom.

The Cardinal's words echoed throughout the stadium:

"For his heroism and his young age, José Sánchez del Río deserves special mention. He was from Sahuayo in Michoacán, and at the age of fourteen he bore valiant witness to Jesus Christ. He was an exemplary son, who shone for his obedience, reverence, and spirit of service. He wanted to be a martyr for Christ from the very beginning of the persecution.

"He shocked those who knew him, for he was so eager to give his blood for Christ. He received the martyr's crown after being tortured and after sending his parents one last message: "We'll see each other in heaven, *Viva Cristo Rey y Santa María de Guadalupe*!"

"The young blessed José Sánchez del Río should inspire us all, especially you young people, who are able to give witness to Christ in your day-to-day life. Dear young people, Christ probably won't ask you to spill your blood, but he certainly does ask you, from today on, to give witness with the truth of your lives in the midst of an environment of indifference to transcendental values and of a materialism and hedonism that attempts to suffocate our consciences. Christ hopes, moreover, for your openness in accepting a vocation prepared for you by him. Only he has the answers to the questions that each of us asks, and he invites you to follow him in married, priestly, or religious life."

Photos

For more photos, visit **blessedjose.com**

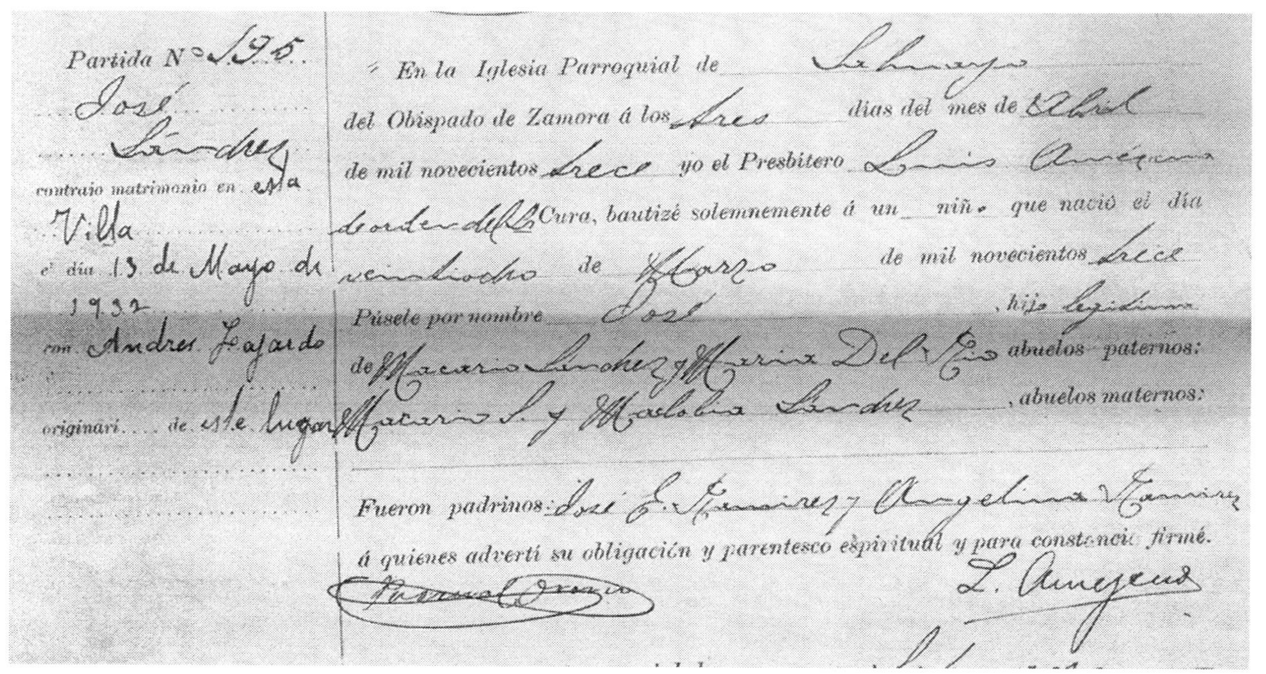

Partida N° 195.
José
Sánchez
contrajo matrimonio en esta
Villa
el día 13 de Mayo de
1932
con Andres Fajardo
originari... de este lugar

En la Iglesia Parroquial de Sahuayo
del Obispado de Zamora á los tres días del mes de Abril
de mil novecientos trece yo el Presbítero Luis Amezcua
de orden del Sr. Cura, bautizé solemnemente á un niño que nació el día
veintiocho de Marzo de mil novecientos trece
Púsele por nombre José, hijo legítimo
de Macario Sánchez y María Del Río abuelos paternos:
Macario S. y Madalena Sánchez, abuelos maternos:

Fueron padrinos: José F. Ramírez y Angelina Ramírez
á quienes advertí su obligación y parentesco espiritual y para constancia firmé.
L. Amezcua

Blessed José's Baptismal Certificate

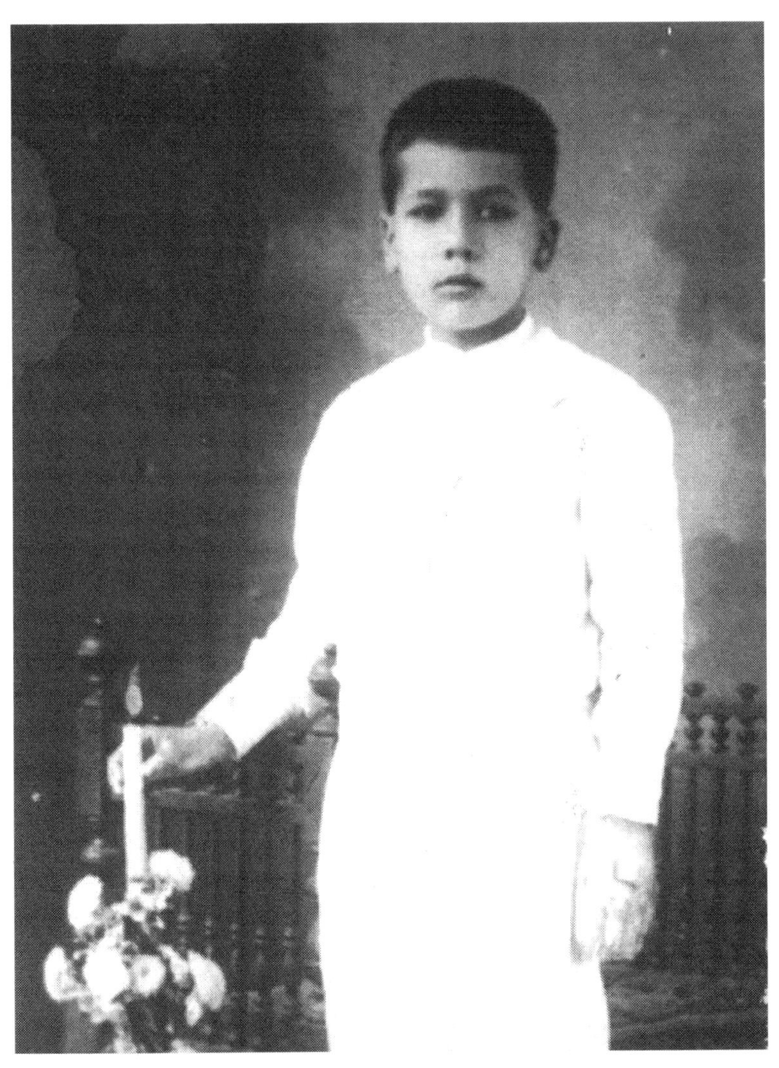

Blessed José at his First Holy Communion

Blessed José's home in Sahuayo on Tepeyac Street. (arrow) In the background is, on the right the parish church of Santiago, in the center the town cemetery, and in the distance the mountains.

Blessed José and Lorenzo after their capture in
Cotija, February 5, 1928
José is on the far left, Lorenzo is next to him

Dup

Cotija Mich. Febrero lunes 6 de 1928.

Sra.María del Rio de Sánchez.
Guadalajara.Jal.

Muy querida mamá:
Fui hecho prisionero en combate en este dia.
Creo que en los momentos actuales voy a morir;pero nada me importa mamá. Resignate a la voluntad de Dios,yo muero contento porque muero en la raya al lado de nuestro Dios.No te apures por mi muerte,que es lo que me mortifica,antes díles a mis otros dos hermanos que sigan el ejemplo que su hermano el mas chico les dejó y túa has la voluntad de Dios,ten valor y mándame la bendición juntamente con la de mi padre.

Salúdame a todos por última vez y tú recibe por último el corazón de tu hijo que tanto te quiere y verte antes de morir deseaba.

José Sánchez del Rio.

Blessed José's message to his mother after his capture, February 6, 1928

Sra
María Sanchez de Olmedo.

Muy querida tia. Estoy sentensiado a muerte a las 8½ se llegará el momento que tanto he deseado te doy las gracias de todos los favores que me isiste tu y Magdalena. No me encuentro capas de escribir a mi mamá tu si me haces el fabor escribe tambien a Maria S. dile a Magdalena que consegui con el teniente me permitiera verla por ultimo, yo creo que no se negara a venir

Saludame a todas y tu recibe como siempre y por ultimo el corazon de tu sabrino que mucho te quiere y verte desea

Cristo vive Cristo Reyna Cristo impera viva Cristo Rey y Santa Maria de Guadalupe.
Jose Sanchez del Rio que murio en defensa de su fe.

No dejen de venir.

Adios.

Letter Blessed José wrote his aunt while in prison
(see page 157)

Place of Martyrdom of Blessed José in the Town Cemetery, Sahuayo - *Notice the Roosters*

Author's Note

This book is the result of ten years of research, during which time I obtained copies of what I believe to be every historical document ever written about José Sánchez del Río.

The main source of information on José's life is the document prepared for his beatification process and given to the Congregation for the Causes of Saints in Rome. It is called a "Positio", and contains a biographical sketch, witnesses' testimony, and anything written by José. My other main sources were the two most extensive books written about José, "Los Gallos de Picazo o los Derechos de Dios" by Father Luis Laureán Cervantes, and "Vida, Muerte, y Beatificatión del Niño Mártir José Sánchez del Río" by Father Javier Villaseñor Castellanos.

We also have a few telegrams written by Federal and Cristero Generals about the three battles and skirmishes in which José took part.

The first was the battle of Los Cutos as described in chapter 24. The second was the raid by Federal troops during Mass as described in chapter 25. The third was his capture during an ambush by Federal troops on February 5, 1928.

I could have used the results of my ten years of research to write a history book. But I wanted the life of Blessed José to come alive for young people like it came alive for me when I first heard his story. So I took all the research I had done and put it together in dramatized form.

We have very few actual quotes from José. Many parts of his life are simply not mentioned by the witnesses. To write a cohesive story, I used everything we have, and then filled in the blanks. Sometimes I relied on local legend, at other times I made connections of my own, and often I just had to put myself in the mindset of a 14-year-old boy again.

All in all, it has been a rewarding adventure. I hope José comes to life in these pages for you, the reader, like he has for me. He is a powerful intercessor and heavenly friend, and an inspiration for us all!

Bibliography

BALL, A., *Young Faces of Holiness,* Our Sunday Visitor, Huntington, 2004, 188-192.

BARRAGÁN DEGOLLADO, A., "Cuando Cerraron los Templos", *Tzacuatl-Ayotl, 14* (1991), 11-16.

CABALLEROS DE COLÓN, *El Mártir de Sahuayo,* 1997.

DE SAN RAMÓN, A., "Jose Sanchez del Rio", *Tzacuatl-Ayotl, 13* (1988),14-20.

FARROW, J., *Pageant of the Popes,* Sheed & Ward, New York, 1942, 391-392.

GARCÍA URBIZU, F., *Zamora y Sahuayo, 1963.*156-161.

GUÍZAR OCEGUERA, J., *Visitas de Ultratumba al Presidente de la Madrid y Episodios de la Guerra Cristera,* Edamex, México D.F., 1983, 146-223.

GUTIÉRREZ, J., *Iosephi Sanchez del Río,* Positio Super Martyrio, Tipografia Nova Res, Roma, 2003.

LAUREÁN CERVANTES, L., *Los Gallos de Picazo o Los Derechos de Dios,* El Arca, México D.F., 1997.

MEYER, J., *La Cristiada,* Siglo XXI, Mexico , 1973, 40.

PARSONS, W., *Mexican Martyrdom,* Tan, Rockford, 1936, 40.

PEREZ VALENCIA, M., *Biografia del "Niño Cristero" Jose Sanchez del Rio.*

PIUS XI, Encyclical Letter *Iniquis Afflictisque,* 1926.

————, Encyclical Letter *Nos es muy Conocida,* 1937.

VILLASEÑOR CASTELLANOS, J., *Vida, Muerte, y Beatificatión del Niño Mártir José Sánchez del Río,* Zamora, 2007.

ZILIANI, L., *Messico Martire,* Amicizia Cristiana, 2012.

Acknowledgements

This book is payment for my debt of gratitude to Blessed José for inspiring me to follow my vocation to the priesthood at the age of 12, probably the best decision I ever made. It was back in 6th grade when a short little seminarian walked into our classroom to substitute-teach religion class. He told us the tale of a 14-year-old Mexican boy who was martyred for his faith and never stopped shouting, "Long live Christ the King!" Blessed José's story got me really riled up, since it was the first time that I realized I too could do something great, even though I was young. Thank you, Brother Eric, for sharing your story with us.

I owe many thanks to my dad, for all his long hours correcting spelling, flow, and story structure. Our little chat on the train to Bibbiano sure helped. Thanks dad!

Many thanks as well to my sister Molly. The cover just wasn't coming together, and then, on the occasion of my first Mass at my home parish of Saint Mary Magdalen in Brentwood, Missouri, she surprised me with a beautiful water color of Blessed José. It was perfect!

To Father Daniel Brandenburg, for your thorough and insightful proofread, I am indebted. Thanks as well to Emilio for all your research, and to Father Joel Castañeda for the photos and stories of life growing up in Sahuayo. Thanks as well to Father Juan Pablo Ledesma, Father Luis Manuel Laureán, Father Nicholas Sheehy, Father Randall Meissen, Father Paul Alger, Father James Perez, and my sister Marianne for their help and advice.

To Father Timothy Walsh, for encouraging me to get the book out there even though it wasn't perfect – your timing was perfect. To Tony Ferraro, for your encouragement and great Cristero impersonations. To Lisa Cusmano, for your marathon proofread – I sure learned a lot about punctuation and capitalization from your dog-eared copy of the book!

I can't forget my mom, who, as I was starting to write, searched high and low for anything written about José for me. Also, for sharing that magical moment back in 1994 when I first heard about José, and everything since, thanks mom!

About the Author

Father Kevin McKenzie is a Catholic priest and a member of the congregation of the Legionaries of Christ. Born in St. Louis, Missouri, he is the third of nine children. He began following God's call to the priesthood at the age of twelve at Immaculate Conception Apostolic School in New Hampshire.

He has spent much of the last 14 years in youth work , first in Connecticut and New York, then later in Ohio, Indiana, and Kentucky.

He started writing this book during his time at Sacred Heart Apostolic School in Indiana, and finished it ten years later during his time in Rome, Italy, studying philosphy and theology. On December 14th 2013, he was ordained a priest at the Basilica of Saint John Lateran in Rome. He is now chaplain at Royalmont Academy, a Catholic school in Cincinnati, Ohio.

He loves writing, reading, ice hockey, helping run boys' summer camps and weekend retreats, guiding pilgrimages, art history, soccer, running, climbing mountains, hiking, cycling, fishing, story-telling, peanut butter cups, photography, cooking, and above all, being a priest.

Contact Father Kevin at **blessedjose.com**